Olive
John Henry's
11th
10th
8th
7th
6th
5th
Oak
Broadway
Coburg
PORTLAND
Patterson
Hilyard
Original Pancake House
Franklin
Nate
Willamette River
Springfield

BETWEEN GEARS™

BY NATALIE NOURIGAT

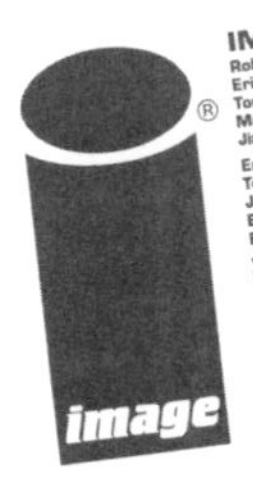
image

IMAGE COMICS, INC.

Robert Kirkman - chief operating officer
Erik Larsen - chief financial officer
Todd McFarlane - president
Marc Silvestri - chief executive officer
Jim Valentino - vice-president

Eric Stephenson - publisher
Todd Martinez - sales & licensing coordinator
Jennifer de Guzman - pr & marketing director
Branwyn Bigglestone - accounts manager
Emily Miller - administrative assistant
Jamie Parreno - marketing assistant
Sarah deLaine - events coordinator
Kevin Yuen - digital rights coordinator
Tyler Shainline - production manager
Drew Gill - art director
Jonathan Chan - senior production artist
Monica Garcia - production artist
Vincent Kukua - production artist
Jana Cook - production artist

www.imagecomics.com

ISBN: 978-1-60706-504-3

BETWEEN GEARS Trade paperback. First Printing. February 2012. Published by Image Comics, Inc. Office of publication: 2134 Allston Way, 2nd Floor, Berkeley, CA 94704. For information regarding the CPSIA on this printed material call: 203-595-3636 and provide reference # EAST – 425928 Printed in the USA. International Rights Representative: Christine Meyer (christine@gfloystudio.com).

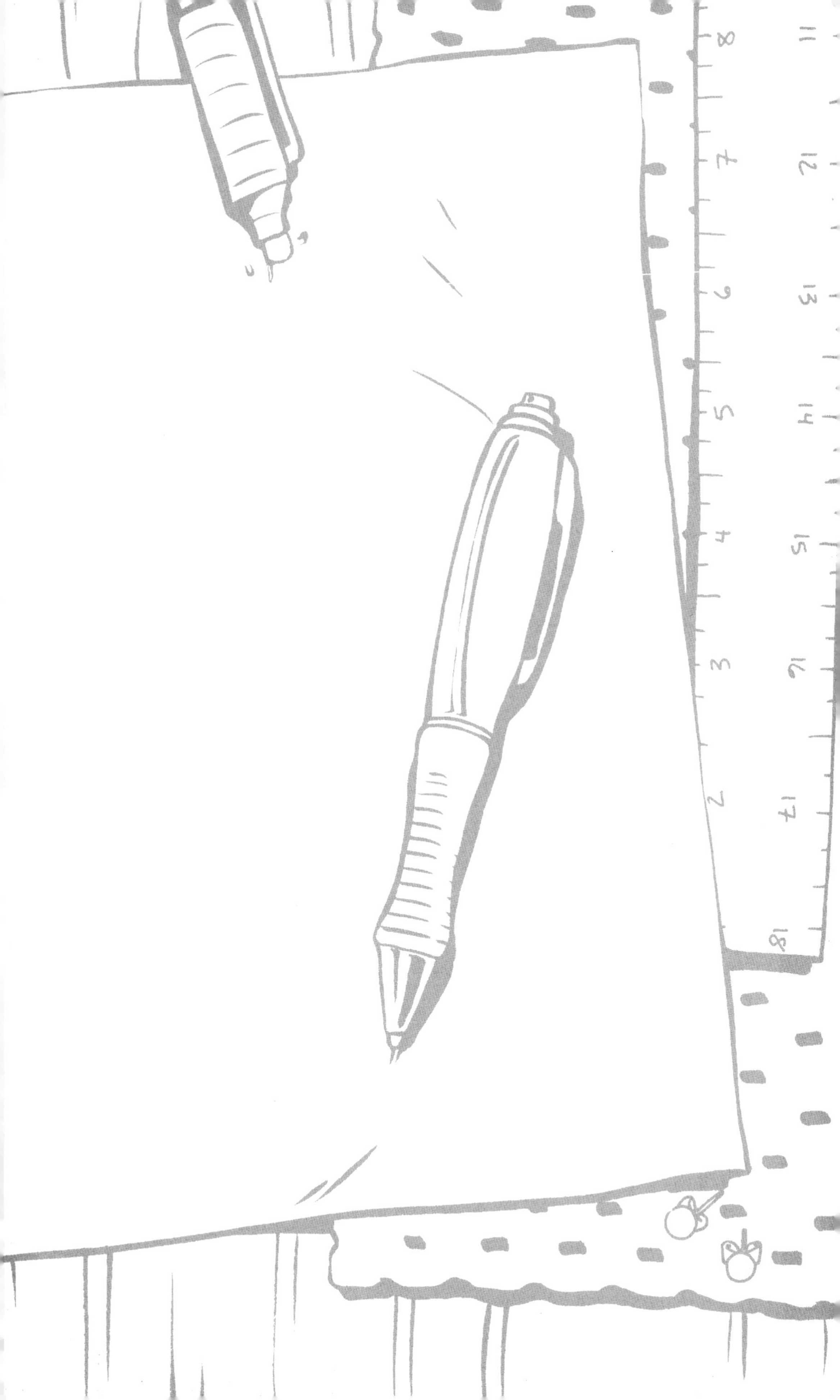

Foreword By
Molly Muldoon

There are some people in your life that you know are truly special. The kind of people that just have a different kind of energy and seem to have a way about them that makes them stand out from the crowd. You already know, just from a few minutes with them, that they are going to *do something*, in italics.

Natalie Nourigat is not one of these people.

Just kidding! Of course she is. From the moment I met her all the way back in our freshman year of high school, I knew that she was something special. Admittedly, I was more excited that there was more than one girl in Japanese Club at that moment but things, obviously, grew from there.

So here we are, years later, and you're about to read Tally's book Between Gears. Can't say I didn't see this day coming but it is just so exciting that it's finally here.

Between Gears, this book you hold in your hands, is the finished product of a few years worth of a lot of work. Somehow, Tally had the wherewithal to record and draw every day of her senior year of college. She covers everything: from nights out to nights of indecision, boys and friends and parties and fights. Nothing is left out and we are invited to view Tally's inner thoughts, something I applaud her on. I know I'm certainly not brave enough to do that.

But here's the problem, friends. Although I'm sure you're about to get a good taste of what Tally thinks about herself, I'd like to start off this book with what others think about Tally. A little background info to get you guys excited.

Here are some things that aren't covered in the book.

The first thing I did when planning this forword was email some of her closest friends to get their views on our poster girl. Although I specifically told them not to be super nice or polite in their descriptions of her (my example quote was "She asks silly questions and has a lot of owl necklaces"), I fear that she must just draw it out of people because that was all I seemed to get.

Cat Farris, a fellow comic booker and Persicope member said, "she's been an inspiration to [her] these past few years." Ron Chan, meanwhile, replied, "Natalie is a rare creature of unusual magnetism and talent. I once heard her described as a glowing fawn and although I have yet to see proof of her iridescence, I am inclined to believe it's a possibility." Although I love Ron's quote, I do have to point out that Tally is not Snape's patronous.

Of course, I didn't just ask Periscope members. Terry, a mutual friend, wrote back that she's "obsessed with Zac Efron and she'll watch almost any show or movie I recommend so, you know, she's a true friend," while a high school buddy, Paul, wrote a non-stereotypical sincere quote: "Beautiful inside and out, Tally channels her endearing personality to her art. She's the best ink bender in the world!"

Pretty high praise, indeed. But do all those pretty words tell you the true story of Natalie Nourigat? I think not. Here are some nuggets of information about Tally that I feel you should know:

+ She used to believe that horses had five hearts, their normal one and then one in each hoof. She was only disillusioned of this belief when she asked about it in the middle of Biology class senior year.

+She's the kind of girl that would spend a weekend making up a science project with you when the two of you had accidently killed the specimens earlier in the month. Not, you know, that that's happened.

+Tally used to draw pictures on her thank you cards and most people I know have kept theirs through the years. I certainly have. Not that I think she's particularly proud of old anime drawings and sketches of us working at video rental stores.

+To that extent, Tally used to draw lots of pictures when she was younger and give them to her parents, so that when she was famous, they could sell them for more money. Always thinking ahead!

+She's the kind of person that will put aside time to talk to you if you're down and will properly apologize if she feels she's done something wrong. Unless you're talking to a-few-drinks!Tally. A-Few-Drinks!Tally could probably care less. And that's why we love her.

+Despite the fact that it was obviously for one person, Tally shared a tent with me on a senior year class trip. We had to keep the flap open so we could both fit and woke up to an experience of authentic morning dew only ever realized by us and fugitives on the run.

+Once we had an arcade all to ourselves for a night and we proceeded to play (and beat) the Jurassic Park game. Upon my complaining that she had shot a Brontosaurus and thus, a good dinosaur, she replied "THERE ARE NO GOOD DINOSAURS!" Something she still believes to this day.

+She would never turn her back on a friend. She is always there to defend. She is the one on whom you can depend! ... No wait, that may be someone else.

The point is, the rumors you've been hearing are true. Natalie Nourigat is a great artist, a great friend and just a great all around person. Have fun getting to know her in Between Gears because you'll be seeing a lot of her in the future.

-Molly, The Girl Who Arrives in A Truck and Makes People Happy

FALL

Thursday, September 17
We just wanted to tell you we love you before you go.
smooch
Aww ♡ I love you guys.
I had so much fun with you this summer!!
I had fun with you, too.
HEY.
Be good this year.
Always is
Dad and Neil surprised me this morning by saying goodbye before they left the house.
Mom and I left for Eugene around 9:00 with my Earthly possessions.
♫ It's time to run the race We're all on the way. Going down the wrong road and it doesn't even matter.
WORDS OF WISDOM
FROM: MOM
I hope you've learned from watching your father that nice people are the ones who really do well in life. They're above being not-nice.
I have to be nicer this year...!!
We spent most of the day unpacking, shopping, setting up furniture, and organizing.
This is why I never buy anything that says 'some assembly required'.
FFFF
huge screw
little hole
...My Studio Designs 'Deluxe Craft Station' was much assembly required.
Niha took me to The Cougar Den to watch Twilight with Cougs Caitlyn, Anna, and Laura.
Ohhhhhh my GOD I'm exhausted.
10:30

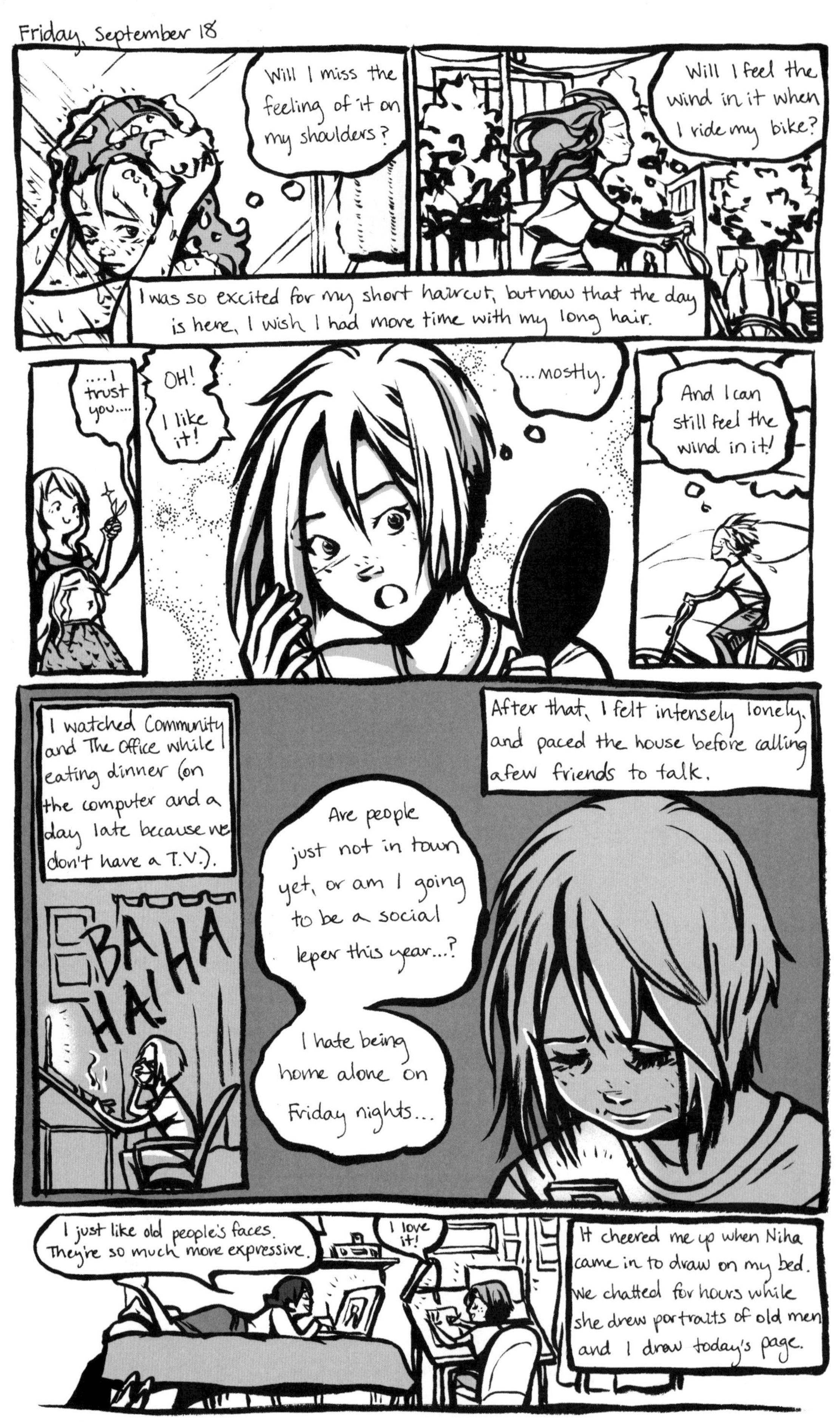
Friday, September 18
Will I miss the feeling of it on my shoulders?
Will I feel the wind in it when I ride my bike?
I was so excited for my short haircut, but now that the day is here, I wish I had more time with my long hair.
....I trust you....
OH! I like it!
...mostly.
And I can still feel the wind in it!
I watched Community and The Office while eating dinner (on the computer and a day late because we don't have a T.V.).
BAHAHA HA!
After that, I felt intensely lonely, and paced the house before calling a few friends to talk.
Are people just not in town yet, or am I going to be a social leper this year...?
I hate being home alone on Friday nights...
I just like old people's faces. They're so much more expressive.
I love it!
It cheered me up when Niha came in to draw on my bed. We chatted for hours while she drew portraits of old men and I drew today's page.

Saturday, September 19
Rain on a tin roof... is not a bad way to wake up.
♑ Capricorn: Today is a day for learning. All you have to do is be sincerely willing to learn.
I'm still getting used to the hair...
WOOSH!
Oh, that's a weird feeling...
NoOooooooooOo.!!
WHAT ARE YOU DOING ?!!!
POOF!
...I have much to learn.
Went to my landlord's restaurant to sign a housing contract and pay rent. He brought me tea and shrimp tempura udon!!!!!!
WOW!!
Thank you SO much!
When Mr. Yi learned that I am a Japanese major, he launched into a Japanese conversation.
ペラペラ?
Que?!!
I've taken a year and a half off from my language studies (thought I would be studying abroad for my remaining credits ....damn you, Economy...), and now I am sufficiently freaked out to resume 400-level courses next week.
I cleaned virtually the entire apartment today.
HN!
15' ceilings gather some epic cobwebs.
TOP
I swept, mopped, spot-cleaned, assembled the dinner table + legs, and reorganized all of the furniture.
Who needs a vacuum cleaner for carpets when you have a broom and elbow grease?
BEAT
TO BOTTOM

Sunday September 20

The neighbors were blasting rap and hip hop at 1... Not just like, "Let's dance to this fun song at our party", but "HAY!! EVERYBODY OUT THERE!!! JUST F.Y.I., THERE'S A PARTY HERE!!!! PLEASE PLEASE PLEASE PLEASE HEAR THIS AND COME!!!!"

Ear plugs

wide awake

getting up at 7

....So I called the police.

....Yes, I am that person.

The reason I got up at 7 on a Sunday? Pi Phi Work Week started today! 9 to 5, baby. Feel the good hurt of sisterhood.

Keeping with tradition, Niha and I took a picture before leaving the house

(AH! I ♥ our new members SO MUCH!!!!)

It was my first time in the house since spring term, and I was terrified to finally see whether or not my forgotten piano music had been tossed.
Thank God, it was all there!

Omigod! Thank you— I tried.

Andy Mangels called to talk about Wonder Woman Day, and mentioned that my piece had been featured on a newsletter of one of the charities.

It will also be in Portland's Lara Sydney Gallery during October!
SO STOKED!!!!

Watching The Emmys at the Cougar Den....
I finished a Tina Fey quote that had cut off early...
"...One time, I walked in on my grandparents having sex, and I didn't leave right away."
...And Anna thought I was serious!!
Oh, wow. How old were you?
HA HA HA HA HA HA HA HA HA HA HA HA HA
?
QUOTE OF THE NIGHT
FROM: NIHA
He's not the voice of my generation...
He's just an egotistical sun-ovagun.

Monday, September 21

We had Work Week activities again today from 9 to 5. As long and tedious as Work Week is, I appreciate that I get this warm-up every year preparing me to make conversation before classes begin.

SOOOOO! How 'bout the weather this week??

Umm... it's good?

I would have to say that despite having so many great, structured events, my favorite memories have been very casual, like watching the LOST premier in the basement with my sisters.

Mm-hm!

I get ~~all~~ most of my awkwardness out now, and know how to be smooth when I'm meeting new people!

I fell asleep on a couch today between meetings...

boop!

hnnn?

...I think I'm getting sick x_x

I watched Garbage music videos for an hour tonight. I love their music, and I love their lyrics, but most of all, I LOVE
Shirley Manson
(DIAGNOSIS: GIRLCRUSH)

I launched Between Gears on Blogspot this evening, and I was so blown-away by the response! Thank you to everyone who linked, retweeted, commented, and e-mailed!
hic!
Matt Grigsby, Erika Moen, Emi Lenox, Hope Larson, Nicolas Hitori de, Jamie Rich, THANK YOU!!

Tuesday, September 22

Woke up sick and decided to stay home from Work Week.
Secret tunnel!! Secre–
-DISMISS-
I counted all of the lights around the house that need new bulbs— NINE!
I thought that it felt dark in here ....
Unfortunately, I can only afford 2 energy-efficient bulbs right now. But I'd rather live in the dark for another month than buy cheap, wasteful bulbs that'll burn out halfway through the year anyway.
N.G.
Bingo
WORDS OF WISDOM
FROM: MY CHOCOLATE WRAPPER
"One's best success comes after one's greatest disappointments."
I've gotta get out there and do something disappointing!
Niha and I live next door to a house where other Pi Phis like to hang out. We can often see them in the window when we come home.

Wednesday, September 23
I woke up with a bad cough this morning, but I couldn't stay home from Work Week again.
On second thought, maybe I like kinkajous best. ♡
Kristen, please host a nature show already.
I'm on Nametag Committee for Work Week, and it is the best one BY FAR! All I do is cut, glue, and chat with the other members.

What?? You're an art major??
Yeah.
Getting to know the new members is great! They are so cool, and I had no idea because I didn't spend time with them last year. I want to be an active senior this year...
Wh—
It was the first day that the gym was open to students, but it closed half an hour before I got there. It was highly anti-climactic.
DAMMIT!
I guess I got a little excercise from riding my bike there...?

I don't know what street I'm on, either!!
Heeey, umm, could I bum, like, 6 of those off you?
Look, I don't know— I thought we just had to walk around and we would find a party!
Well I'm about this close to jusk knocking on doors.
The freshmen were on campus today, and they are OUT TONIGHT! I saw so many UO sweatshirts, baseball caps, Pabst packs, and American Eagle jeans today, man.... And now they're walking up and down my street, looking for a party and making noise. It makes me laugh, but God, I remember those days. I didn't know how to dress, get alcohol, learn about the cool parties before they happened... It's tough being a freshman.

Thursday, September 24

The senior class crashed Pi Phi at 8:00 this morning and woke up the sophomores for a surprise breakfast together!

COFFEE
DONUTS

Seniors had it easy today in Work Week... I drew for two hours while waiting around.

Right now I'm practicing drawing the Loch Ness monster for Emerald City Comicon's "Monsters & Dames" book.

oOOOOOOo

I learned how to use a lighter today, and had an EVE moment when it suddenly ignited.

Went to 80's Night at Henny's with dorm friends Hannah, Dana, Christina, Lauren, and Michelle.

WHEE!

Hannah's roommate Daneille gave us a lift downtown.

WO-OA
LIVING ON A PR

It was really fun, and I knew the words to more songs than I usually do at the bars, haha.

Friday, September 25
Today, Pi Phi had mock recruitment with Alpha Phi, meaning that we visited their house as pretend-Potential New Members, and they did the same for us. Walking across town as a 100-person group in sorority letters is kind of embarrassing.
ΑΦ
It's good to spend time with members of other houses, because you see pretty soon that, actually, you have a lot in common!
We had a Work Week party tonight with a 'yachting' theme. I wish I had brought my costume drawer to school...
The pool boys in Chabo were just darlings this year, no?
Speaking of costumes, it's almost time to pick a Halloween costume! My favorite ideas right now are Gilly or Angie Tempura from SNL, or Dwight from The Office.
Sorry.
Bitch, please!!
SNAP! SNAP!
Bears.
Beets.
Battlestar Galactica.

Saturday, September 26

DER NER NER NER
DRUM DRUM
GRRRRR...

I was on hold with Adobe for over an hour today... This is the 4th time I've called this week, and it always takes so long that I give up before reaching a real person, but today I stuck with it for 75 minutes, and finally got Ann!

In the mean time, I drew for about 8 hours today, and simultaneously watched Parks & Recreation, Community, Dollhouse, The Office, Bones, SNL, Glee, and Fringe on my computer.

SOOOO great...

Even though our football team beat Cal 42-3, and it was the Saturday night before school starts, my block was silent all night! Shocking! I slept really well!

Oh, thank you, Jesus.

Sunday, September 27

Work Week was a LOVE FEST today. We took 2 hours to just spontaneously compliment anyone that we wanted to in front of the group.
You wouldn't steal, like, a Gummi Bear.
I'm starting to think that you don't have, like, a bad thought in your mind.
Uhh, funny story from when I worked in a candy store...
I'm trying to befriend all of the cats in my alley before the end of the year. I've given them all nicknames, and so far....
MOW!
...Pumpkin is my BFF.
HISS
...Biscuit hates me.
?
...And Mangey freaks me out. (I'll leave you food, but I won't pet you....)
There is the coolest looking cat at the end of the alley. It's all white with a solid black tail.
I shall call her 'Snowy', and she shall be mine, and she shall be my Snowy.
Whatever you do, do it with confidence.
You are doing the right thing
In the right place
At the right time.

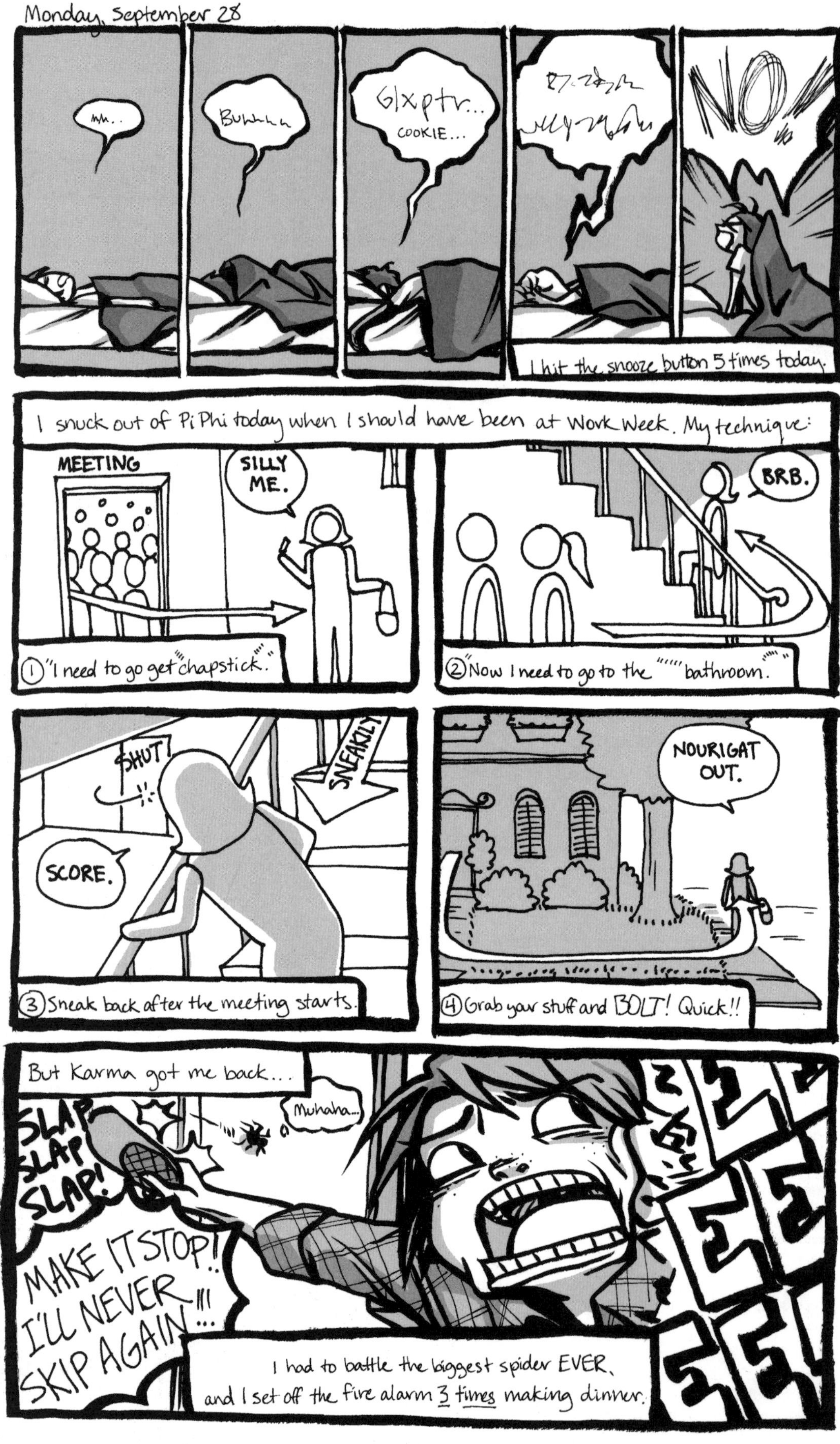
Monday, September 28
Mm..
Buhhhh
Glxptr...
COOKIE...
NO!
I hit the snooze button 5 times today.
I snuck out of Pi Phi today when I should have been at Work Week. My technique:
MEETING
SILLY ME.
① "I need to go get "chapstick."
BRB.
② "Now I need to go to the "bathroom."
SHUT!
SNEAKILY
SCORE.
③ Sneak back after the meeting starts.
NOURIGAT OUT.
④ Grab your stuff and BOLT! Quick!!
But Karma got me back...
Muhaha...
SLAP SLAP SLAP!
MAKE IT STOP!! I'LL NEVER SKIP AGAIN!!!...
I had to battle the biggest spider EVER, and I set off the fire alarm 3 times making dinner.

Tuesday, September 29
FIRST DAY OF SCHOOL!!
My last one, in fact. How strange to think....
実は、この授業を二年前取りましたが…その間にはとても下手になってしまいました…
Spoken Japanese: not bad for a 2-year hiatus!
— Starbucks Intermission —
old friend
new friend?
はい、この漢字を読んで下さい。
......
But written Japanese? HELLA SCARY.
= YOU
History of Superheroes: AHUHUHUH! So happy that I live in a decade when this is actually a class you can take.
Shit, calm down. It's DAY ONE.
Stupid freshmen...

Wednesday, September 30

puffy face....

I woke up groggy, even though I got 11 hours of sleep. Maybe I should get my tonsils out after all...

It was the first day of class for 'Little Magazines', an elective about the history of Modernist periodical magazines.
100-year-old zine!!
OOOOOOOO...

The homework for written Japanese took me 2 hours!! But studying kanji is so cool... Even though each symbol can have several meanings, and combining symbols makes endless new meanings, they make sense in the strangest ways! Sometimes I feel like Lyra, trying to understand the Alethiometer.

洞察...
The symbols for 'cave' and 'investigate'.... that could mean—! 'To discern'!

I really don't get how you come to these conclusions....

Y-you know! Like, if I investigate a cave, I can... discern... the darkness?...

Thursday, October 1
Between classes, I went to the top of Friendly Hall to look for my thesis advisor.
HUFF
HUFF
HUFF
She wasn't there, but I had a free hour, so I explored the hall. It ended with an ancient door to the fire escape.
Score! no fire alarm!
The sun was out, I was reading The Superman Chronicles for the first time, and I had a cool spot to myself. It was an instant memory.
Welcome!
And HOW!!
YES, YES!
Went to Amelie's house for an epic vegan, garden-enthusiast dinner event, and what an event it was! Music! Dancing! Cooking! Wine!
CHIK CHIK CHIK
....Other things I can't mention!
Thank you...! I will enjoy that... visually. From over here.
HA
HA
HA
HA
HA!
HA!
HEH
Mmm-well, to be fair, Jim... James. Jimothy?
HAHAHA HA HA HA! HA
Kayla invited me over to watch The Office at her house. It was so wonderful to see her again! We lived together sophomore year, but only get little windows of time anymore.

Friday, October 2

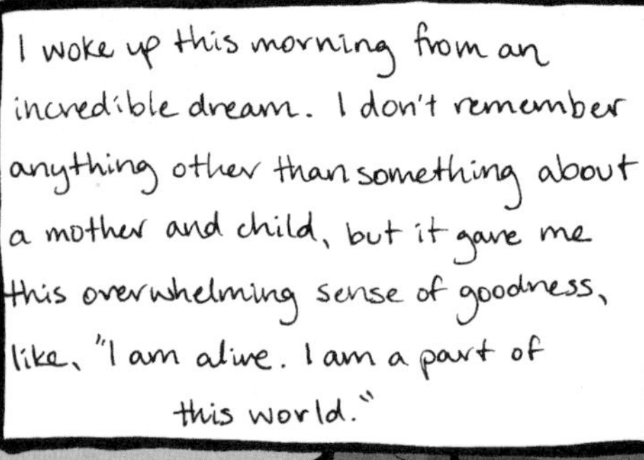
I woke up this morning from an incredible dream. I don't remember anything other than something about a mother and child, but it gave me this overwhelming sense of goodness, like, "I am alive. I am a part of this world."
Marble, but represent real people
I moved the baby closer to its mother, like this.

CARE PACKAGE
2 SKIRTS!
GRANOLA BARS!
SHOES!
AND A SWEET NOTE ♥
Thank you, Mom!
FROM HOME!

While stretching at the gym, I noticed that I have spider veins starting by my ankles.
I felt sorry for myself, until I made eye contact with a woman with muscular dystrophy. She smiled at me brightly, as if to say, "Bodies rock. Fuck the details."

Saturday, October 3
24-HOUR COMIC DAY!
Curses! Foiled again! Someday, I WILL participate...!!
...But I have other plans...
Visual journaling seminar!
Do you have a ticket to the game?
No. I'm not exactly a hard-core Duck football fan.
Oh...well, I was going to say that we're going to Dylan's to watch the game and order pizzas, but...
...
....Let me clarify: under the right conditions and with the right people, I'm a Duck football fan.
Dylan's Epic Hat

Sunday, October 4
Visual journaling seminar concludes!
Instructions: Take a walk and pick up 2 items — one natural and one human trash. Then, journal about your walk and create a design combining the items.
tree pod thingers
branch
coffee cup heat guard (unfolded)
My finished sketchbooks suck. I am okay with being a sucky bookmaker... I've always been too impatient with crafts...
Actually, that class has been hard, too...
It was a tough week, to be honest. I didn't realize until I recounted it to my family during our weekly phone call.

Monday, October 5
Midnight: 2010 JET applications are up!! Where is my life going?? Where will I be next fall??!
Oh SNAP! Here comes the real world...!
Amélie looked out the window during class today, and I noticed how loud her watch is.
Tick Tock Tick Tock Tick Tick Tock Tick Tock
Am I the only one who can hear that?
I don't have to see her face— I know what she's thinking.
Tick Tock
Tick Tock
Tick Tock
I think that every senior in the room can hear the watch.
It was a joke this summer, but the hard times are here.
THESIS
My super-serious senior year is off to a super-serious start.

Tuesday, October 6

Photoshop finally works! Praise Allah!

I can use pressure sensitivity to tone again!

My primary thesis advisor had tons of great feedback and ideas for me in our meeting today, but I still left very concerned about my thesis. It just seems so vague right now...

tap

That's normal!

I do my Pi Phi duties, I do my homework, I eat, I sleep.
There's nothing left at the end of the day.

Wednesday, October 7

Little Magazines took a trip to Special Collections and looked at real, original little magazines from the late 1800s and early 1900s!

There was the coolest one, called 'Young England,' which was pretty much 'The Dangerous Book for Boys,' 1914 edition. Epiiiic.... They had stories like 'Canadian Moose Attack!' and dated, super-srs illustrations of ridiculous things.
Like moose attacks.

I volunteered at the street fair, and it was really fun!

VOLUNT

Hannah ran into me, and she says that there will be a thesis support group! Hallelujah! I could use support!

AVACADOD
...omagaud.
Tonight was our last practice before recruitment. Everyone looks so tired...

Niha is 21!!
I think I'm actually just going to go to bed...
Aww, really?
We could both probably use the sleep.

Thursday, October 8
Recruitment starts today!! Best face forward! I am showered, makeup'd, and generally cutified.
You got your hair done and your nails done, too, a new outfit and your Fendi shoes!
Even my huge, stupid bag can't hold all of my things today. It is literally overflowing with my responsibilities.
My secret weapons today are:
instant coffee
eye drops
Aleve
1
2
3
WELCOME TO PI BETA PHI'S OPEN HOUSE!!

Friday October 9

A flock of scrub jays woke me up unceremoniously this morning...

SQUAK.

Hey.

HAY.

SQUAK!

Get out of here!! SHOO!!

Meow!

Meow! Meow!

HISSSS!!!

RAWR!!

SQUAK

They're unflappable... I wonder how feasible it would be to get a slingshot in case this happens again....

Living with another person really serves as a foil to your true nature.
I thought I was casual about messes, but this...

Recruitment continues! I can't let you in on this one, but basically we were just waiting around after 10:00 for a super-double-secret (probation) meeting to begin...

...And since we hadn't even STARTED by midnight, and it lasts 3-4 hours, I went home and went to sleep.

UGH.

Saturday, October 10

Turns out that that 'super double-secret meeting' last night started at 1 A.M. and ran until 4 A.M. I have been a member for 3 years, I have put in my time, and I refuse to do ridiculous things for Pi Phi anymore. 4 A.M.?!

Ridiculous... ridiculous!!

We have the cutest outfits EVVVERR for philanthropy day. ♡

Girls! Hey! I know you're tired, but get pumped up!

You're soldiers!!

This is Sparta!!

THIS IS SPARTA!!

HA-OO HA-OO!

...OKAY! But we're quiet Spartans!

PFFF!!

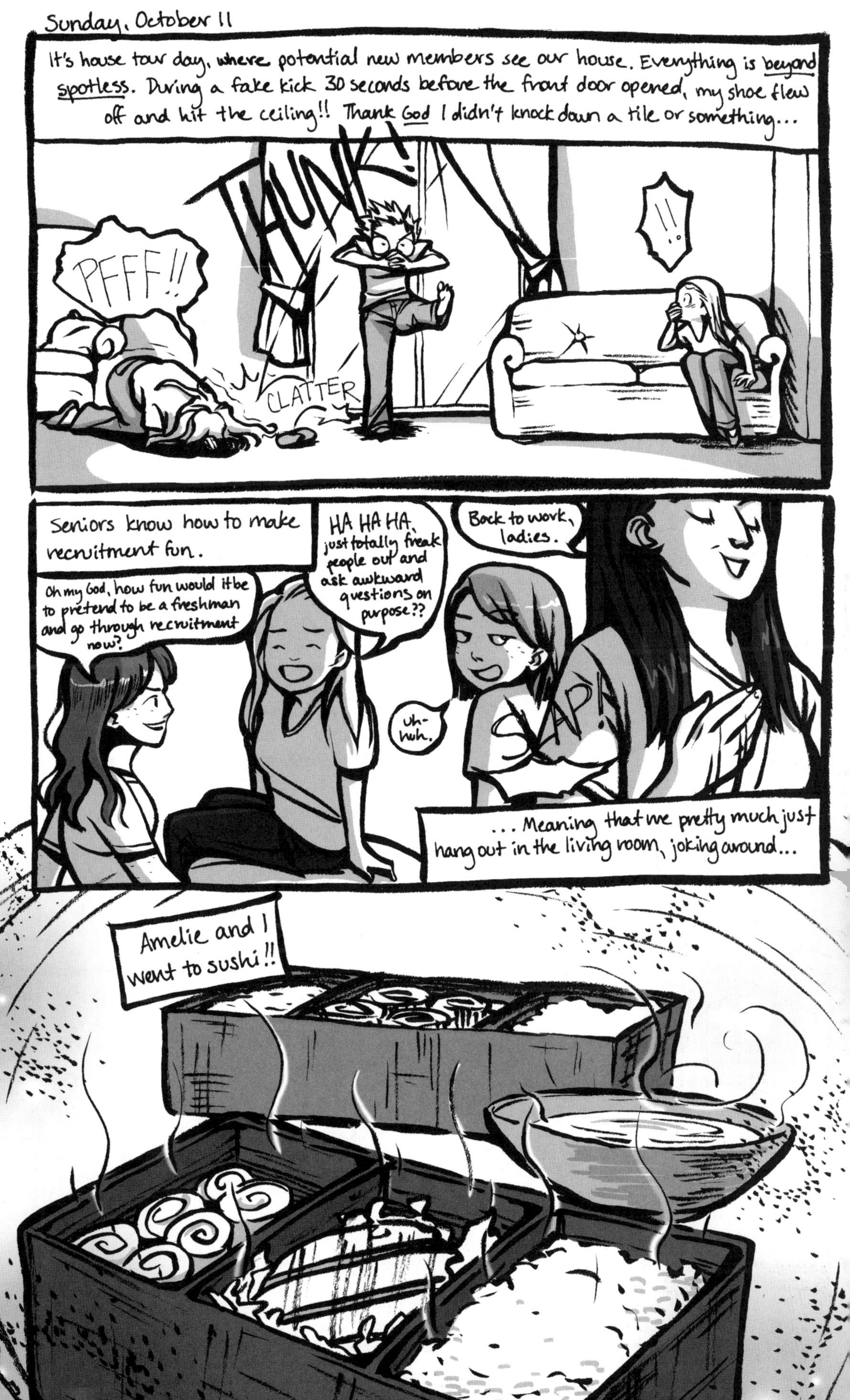
Sunday, October 11
It's house tour day, where potential new members see our house. Everything is beyond spotless. During a fake kick 30 seconds before the front door opened, my shoe flew off and hit the ceiling!! Thank God I didn't knock down a tile or something...
THUNK!
PFFF!!
!!
CLATTER
Seniors know how to make recruitment fun.
Oh my God, how fun would it be to pretend to be a freshman and go through recruitment now?
HA HA HA, just totally freak people out and ask awkward questions on purpose??
Uh-huh.
Back to work, ladies.
SLAP!
...Meaning that we pretty much just hang out in the living room, joking around...
Amelie and I went to sushi!!

Monday, October 12
SOOOO SICKKKK... Sorest throat EVER. Niha has swine flu. It was always just a matter of time, but now...
SPLITTING HEADACHE
Oh... my God...
I need to go get some water...
ARGGG!! This drinking fountain has never worked, not since I got here 3 years ago!!! How hard is it to fix a damn drinking fountain?!!?
...It's the little things that break you.
Recruitment from 5 to 10. I play piano and sneeze on people.

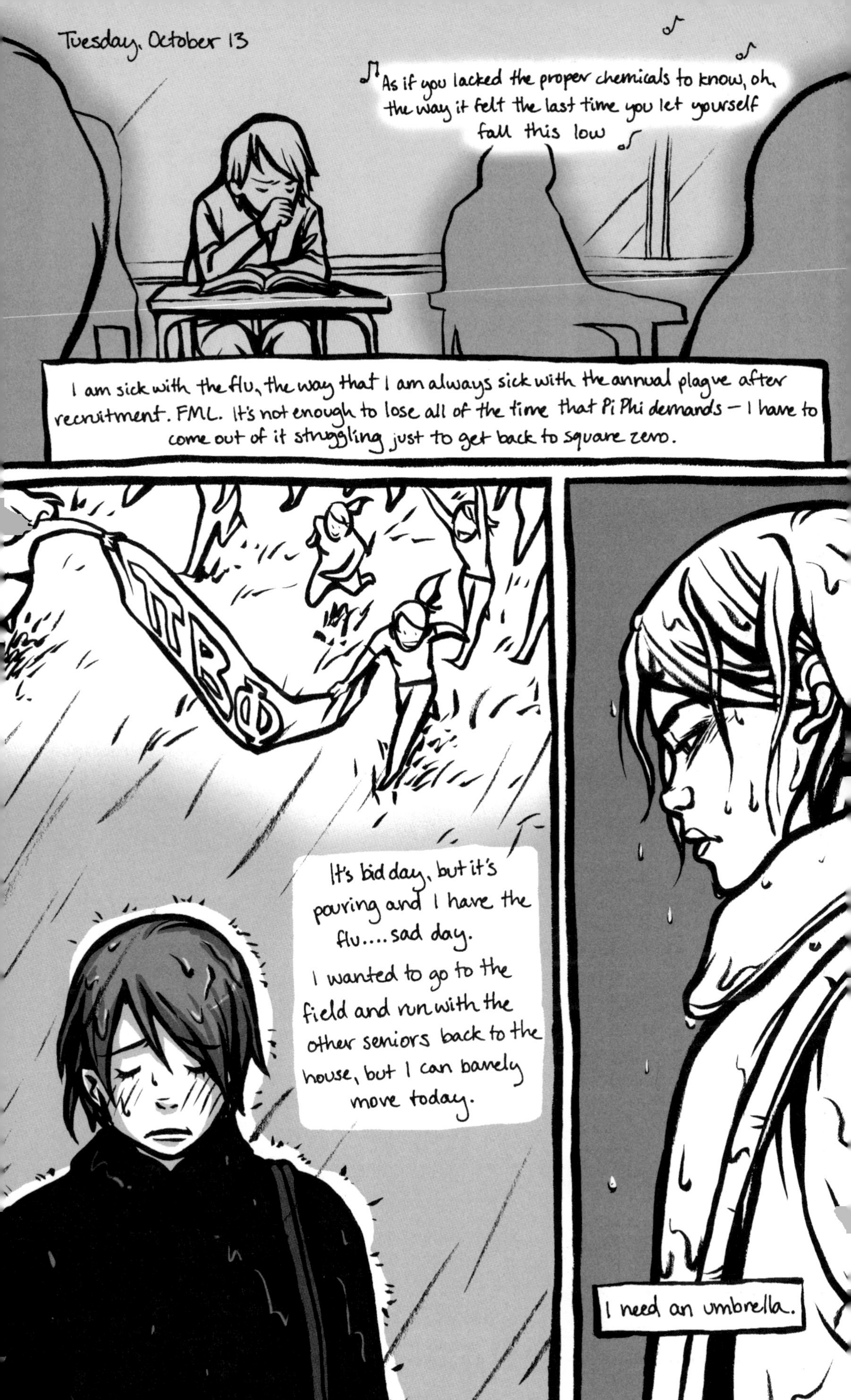
Tuesday, October 13
As if you lacked the proper chemicals to know, oh, the way it felt the last time you let yourself fall this low
I am sick with the flu, the way that I am always sick with the annual plague after recruitment. FML. It's not enough to lose all of the time that Pi Phi demands — I have to come out of it struggling just to get back to square zero.
ΠΒΦ
It's bid day, but it's pouring and I have the flu.... sad day.
I wanted to go to the field and run with the other seniors back to the house, but I can barely move today.
I need an umbrella.

Wednesday, October 14
I have the flu and feel feverish. Things are hard to remember......fuzzzy....
And furthermore, I will be needing... cookies.
...
I stayed home all day except for a much needed grocery run. I looked like something that the tide dragged in.
I ate Doritos and passed out for 6 hours.

Thursday, October 15

I may have the flu, but that doesn't mean that anyone else has to get it from me.

Senior Night at Taylor's!

...And then a house party with the new members...
YAAAAAAAAA!!

...I drunkenly hailed my first pedicab to avoid walking through town with a half-finished 6-pack of Smirnoff Ice.
Haaaaaaaaayy!!
How far will you take me for ... one dollar??

He ended up taking me all 10 blocks home!
You know, I can also pay you in Smirnoff Ices...!
I don't think that's a good idea...
Even in the course of the half block remaining, 3 separate groups heckled me about the alcohol!!!

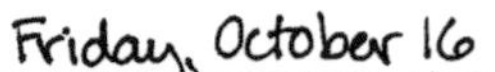
Friday, October 16

I am still struggling miserably in written Japanese. I am very competitive, especially in school, and being in the bottom half of the class is unbearable! I refuse to stay down here!

I tried to nap again, but I was just lying in bed thinking.
I really should do that thing.

I read Wonder Woman for the first time! The Greatest Stories Ever Told and The Circle.

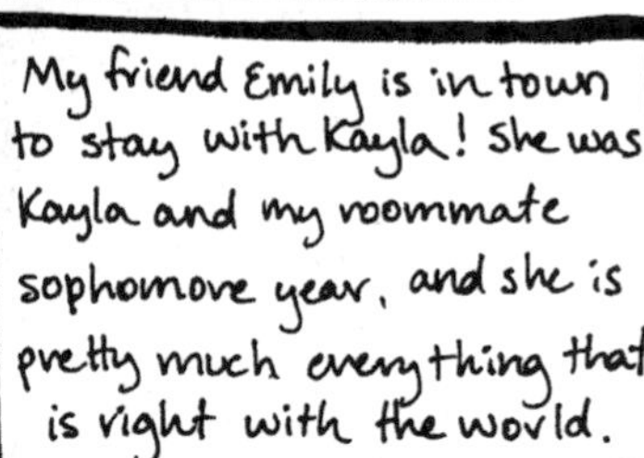
My friend Emily is in town to stay with Kayla! She was Kayla and my roommate sophomore year, and she is pretty much everything that is right with the world.

SMART
FUNNY
SWEET
PRETTY (sexy, let's be honest)
CARING

HIRE A DOG, TO BURN DOWN A HOSPITAL!!
whaaat.
SLOTHS!

You know~ she's the white one on that show!
Omigod, I miss our trifecta.

Saturday, October 17

After so many years of drawing, even the repetitive task of prepping paper for comics has become familiar and soothing, like meditation. I spent hours today happily ruling sheets of Bristol board to music.

I showered, did my hair and makeup, cleaned, went grocery shopping... and I have 5 hours until the party tonight to do as I please! This is a good day!

FREETIME

GIRLS' NIGHT OUT VERSION 3.0!

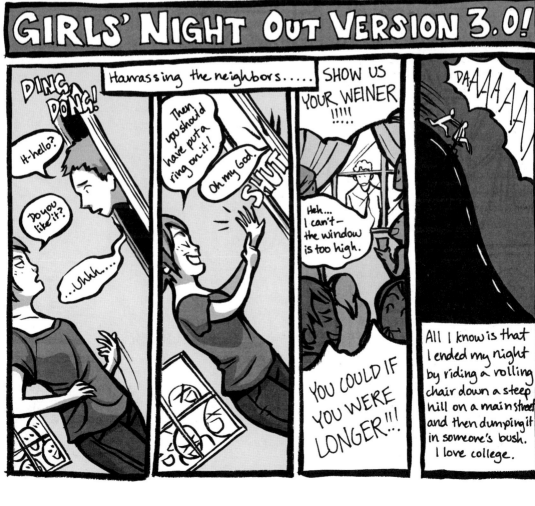

Harrassing the neighbors.....

DING DONG!

H-hello?

Do you like it?

...Uhhh....

Then you should have put a ring on it!

Oh my God.

SHUT

SHOW US YOUR WEINER !!!!!

Heh... I can't- the window is too high.

YOU COULD IF YOU WERE LONGER!!!...

DAAAAAA

All I know is that I ended my night by riding a rolling chair down a steep hill on a main street and then dumping it in someone's bush. I love college.

Sunday, October 18
Hangover brunch with Hannah and Christina at Café Sienna!
THESIS
THESIS
Mrf-mm!
I got my first breakfast burrito EVER and LOOOVED it.
Hannah and I spent hours in the library, but in the end all that I accomplished was inking and scanning my piece for ECCC's Monsters & Dames book, and making a budget for next year's cons and the materials I need to buy.
Actually studying
Just a poser
Let's go, Elasmosaurus-type thing! We can do it!!
MAA!
Monsters & Dames drawing~~!!
My digital coloring skills leave something to be desired, but no one ever got better by hiding from the things they weren't good at.

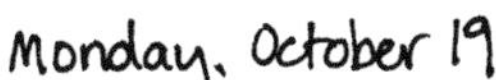
Monday, October 19

I drew for hours today, but it feels like I'm just spinning my wheels in the dirt. Will I ever get ahead on these projects?

More Wonder Woman readin' times♥

Molly and I complained to each other over the internet about how hard school is and our growing senioritis.
Is it too late to apply to Hogwarts?
Yeah. Like 11 years too late.
...What about Pigfarts?
Ha ha ha ha.
OMG Molly I'm so serious right now.

Tuesday, October 20
The huge trees covering the UO pathways are dropping acorns this week - you could get a concussion from the way those things rocket down! I channeled Wonder Woman and played bullets and bracelets with a few today, trying not to die by acorn.
PEW PEW!
THUNK
shit.
...
I didn't leave time to eat lunch before leaving for class today. By the time I was done at 6:30, I was actually bumping into walls while walking and talking with a professor. so... weak....
My bike is safe after being locked up in an unfamiliar parking lot for 3 days!
where the fuck have you been?!
HUZZAH!
Molly may come and visit this weekend!
HUZZAH!

Wednesday, October 21
Sorry I'm late.
That's alright. Is it still raining pretty hard out there, then...?
...yeah.
Jan
Feb
March
April
May
June
July
Aug
Sep
Oct
N...
(finals)
(finals)
3
2
1
0
CUPS PER DAY
My coffee habits wax and wane in perfect time with my stress level.
Oh cruel mistress! Lend me your dark powers!!
Today, I was so overwhelmed by how behind I am on art projects that...
I slipped up to 2 cups per day.

Thursday, October 22
2 months away from my 22nd birthday! 2,2,2,2,2,2!!
Fall is my mom's favorite season because everything is so colorful, and it's a time of year when a lot of new things are starting for people (school, sports).
I've always liked fall the least, because it feels like everything is dying. This year, though, I see fall the way that my mom does. My dad had heart surgery this summer, and the fact that he's still with us makes this fall feel like a celebration of life.
My friend Kyle walked me home, and we talked about everything from Japanese to Halloween to 2012. What is it about me that makes guys want to talk about the apocalypse....?
?
My Japanese essay was so frustrating, I had to solve my Rubik's cube to feel confident in my intelligence again.
Suck it!

Friday, October 23
Today was one huge rain storm. I was late getting out the door, so I had to bike to class, and my hood wouldn't stay down. Later, my bike lock broke!
Take that, Sakubun.
SLAP!
BEEP BEEP
!!
That Molly girl came to visit!
I do like that Molly girl. ♡
Sushi dinner!
Shopping!
Ho ho ho~~!
AAH!!
The Vampire's Assistant!
She's... BEAUTIFUL!
PFFF
Video blog!
...What to say.
Really though.

Saturday, October 24

Understanding Superheroes Conference at the UO! Molly and I went and listened to 3 speakers: Kurt Busiek, Gail Simone, and Matt Fraction. It was fun and informative — the speakers were congenial and funny, as so many comic folk are.

I got Gail to sign The Circle!
...And then ran away, because I am ridiculously shy sometimes.

Molly and I had creative times in my room, interspersed with T.V. shows. The original Inspector Gadget show's soundtrack is totally rock-outable, for the record.

GO,

GADGET,

GO!

Sunday, October 25

Thanksgiving.
...Thanksgiving.
Goodbye, Molly!!! ;_;

Inked with Mononoke Princess in the background.
Look, everyone! This is what hatred looks like!

Researched seriously in the library for my thesis.

I called my good friend Mary to talk while I walked to the grocery store. She goes to school in D.C., and I almost always forget the time difference and wait too long in the day to call her, but not today!

Monday, October 26

I can do this, I can DO this!
I read other theses today in the HC library.

A classmate was presenting in class, and asked me to wait at the door of the building to show her advising professor to the right room. He came a different way, and she forgot to send someone for me!

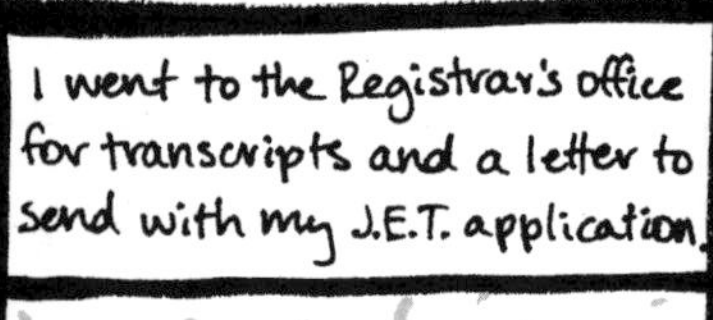
I went to the Registrar's office for transcripts and a letter to send with my J.E.T. application.

I feel a little bit better with those steps done, but there is still so much to get together...!

Do I deserve sushi?
I deserve sushi!
DO IT!
why?!

I treated myself to chicken katsu and California rolls at Sakura's. I'm realizing where all of my spending $ goes...

I watched Porco Rosso and read an article on it for my thesis. Combining work and play is the best!
ポルコ、本当はスパイなの？

Tuesday, October 27
I saw a hummingbird flitting around the roof of the library out of the corner of my eye. I love that building — I see something new and magical every time I go.
I finally went to the Jordan Schnitzer Museum of Art's Superheroes collection! Hundreds of thousands of dollars in original art dating back to the 1920s. It is a glorious, glorious thing.
I just got a commission for a Darwyn Cooke-style Cat-woman, and what do you know? The collection had a Cooke cat-woman cover!! You can bet I stared for a while.
First meeting of my children's book illustration class!! I took down some ideas and sketches for a story idea, and people were so nice walking by and commenting on them!
Oookay. so I'm going to write my story, and you can draw it!
Oh! She looks like a Ghibli character!

Wednesday, October 28

Heh, classic.
Klik!

Oooh, foggy moon...
EE EE EE EE!
EE!
zip!
And bats!

Oh fer— you're 3 days early!!

Thursday, October 29
It's about Buddha and Jesus getting an apart-ment together in Tokyo.
That.
Sounds.
Amazing.
Must read: Saint Young Men
+ Vintage top and skirt
+ Glue, magnets, pipe cleaner, and ping pong balls
HIRON'S
+ Paper mache, superglue, duct tape, and 4 hours
3:30 A.M.
TA
BAD WOBOT!
DA

Friday, October 30
Riding the train to Portland beside the Willamette River... so beautiful!
Is it sad that ivy growing over rusty bridges and abandoned cranes makes me nostalgically proud of Oregon...?
I so prefer the train to the bus. It's a smooth ride, so I can read and draw. Instead of the highway, we travel through farms and by the river. I get leg room, a tray, can keep my bag with me, can walk around, and there's a freaking OBSERVATION DECK with swiveling chairs! Straight pimpin'.
MEDICINE-FRIDAY!
GOOD Ol' Times!
Matt...I set off the fire alarm ...!!
It's OK!
Shanghai Tunnels
THIS. IS THE BEST THING EVER EVER.
I kno rite.
bacon-wrapped, cheese-stuffed dates
Martini Bar
酔っ払い!
DRUNKY-DRUNK!
Sushi Time

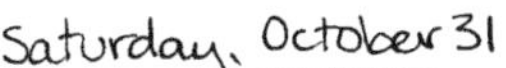
Saturday, October 31

Watched What Not to Wear and South Park with Mom and Nick.

SKETCH GROUP!!! I missed it so bad
Between Gears
Emitown
Hilarious Tin-Tin Parody

Carved a pumpkin with grandma, Dad, and Mom.

I just prefer watching from home. I don't want to be sitting next to someone shouting— Oh, OH! TOUCHDOWN! OOOOOOOH!!!
Watched the Ducks totally own the Trojans.

TRICK OR TREAT!
Oh, wow! OK, now you all have a choice... You can have tasty, healthy celery, or candy....
We're not creepers, just easily amused!
CANDY!
CANDY!
...Candy?
What?! Candy?? Well, if that's what you want...
My Dad is so good with kids. I can't wait to see what he's like as 'Grandpa'.

Halloween on Hawthorne #14!

Sunday, November 1

HUNG OVER
Ooooog...

New Facebook photos from last night
WH AT
When the hell did I think that pose was a good idea?!

Golf practice with Dad.

Target trip with Mom.
bad habit of walking behind her like a duckling

So, if you had a lot of small projects to do on your house, would you do them all at once to save on costs...?
That's a very good question, Neil!
What is going on..? More than 10 words out of Neil in one conversation?
Family dinner at P.F. Chang's before dropping me off at the train station. An unusual family dynamic lately...

My parents gave me money to take a taxi home from the station! Such a luxury ♡

Monday, November 2

I missed class today... My books were so ridiculously expensive that I didn't even buy them all, and I don't want to go if I didn't do the reading...
Guilty
I checked out 4 books for my thesis and started pulling quotes for the paper. I need to decide what I want the art portion to be about. I estimate that I will have time for a 48-page story... so how do I make something meaningful in that length of a comic...?
super-srs thinking mode
Big cleaning day: laundry, sweeping, dishes.
Japanese midterm TOMORROW!!!!!!!!
影響…影響…
影響影響影
響影響影響!!!!...
only 7 more months of this lifestyle!!

Tuesday, November 3
56 kanji compounds to remember on the midterm today... can I do it?!
There's something about walking quickly, reading a sheet of paper furiously, and muttering to yourself that makes people curious.
Midterm Self-Assessment:
I'm putting my money on a 90%. I felt confident on all but 2 questions, but I do make little mistakes that cost me...
MMM YES
If you flip back page by page from the center of chapter V, what do you notice? It's symmetrical!
Oooooh...
WHAAAT!!
My mind = blown
We talked about Watchmen in comics class today. These comics are interesting when you read them on your own, but getting an English major lecture on them reveals so much more.
Children's book class: Still awesome! I rediscovered The Boy Who Drew Cats, a wonderful, scary story from my childhood.
It's the first art style that I remember studying and trying to copy on my own; everything I drew in 1996 was that fluid feline silhouette.
the little Natalie

Wednesday, November 4

Decompressed with Amélie in Little Magazines class.
Things have been CRAZY.
I KNOW.
NOD
(Has 10X the responsibility I do, including a student gov't position)

I bought Darwyn Cooke Catwoman issues and read them once for enjoyment, once to study his art style.

flip

Like this?

I spent one hour on a term paper, one hour on my thesis. I can do bite-sized tasks.

This fashionable man I know by sight popped out in front of me in a long hallway. I got to follow his boots and short pants all the way down the hallway. Some kind of male-type magic kept me from looking away from the boots.

Monday, October 26

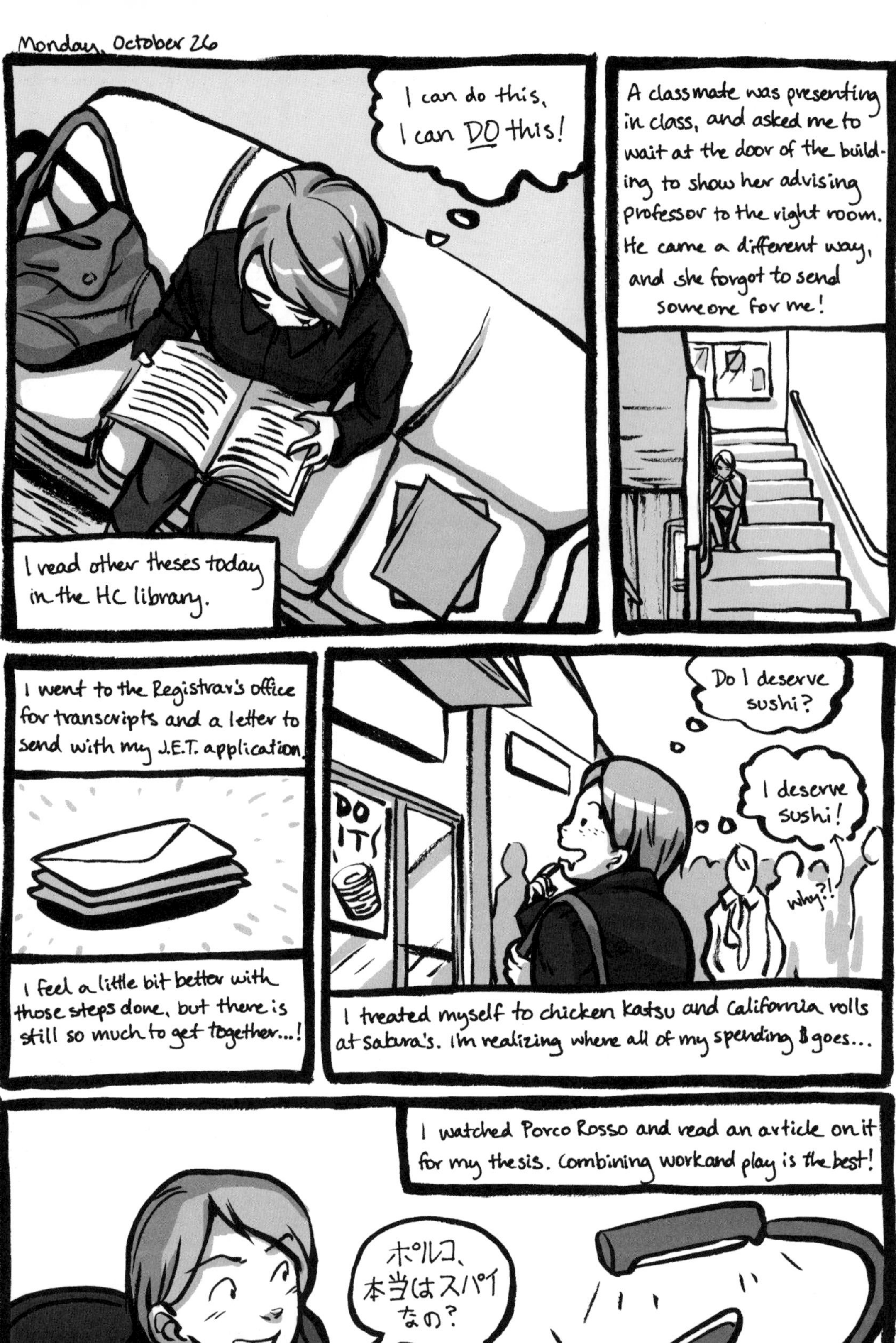
I can do this, I can DO this!
I read other theses today in the HC library.
A classmate was presenting in class, and asked me to wait at the door of the building to show her advising professor to the right room. He came a different way, and she forgot to send someone for me!
I went to the Registrar's office for transcripts and a letter to send with my J.E.T. application.
I feel a little bit better with those steps done, but there is still so much to get together...!
DO IT
Do I deserve sushi?
I deserve sushi!
why?!
I treated myself to chicken katsu and California rolls at Sakura's. I'm realizing where all of my spending $ goes...
I watched Porco Rosso and read an article on it for my thesis. Combining work and play is the best!
ポルコ、本当はスパイなの？

Friday, November 6

I worked on the story for my thesis comic. I was going to just revamp an old story, but I fleshed out one of the side characters to the point that I decided the story should be about her. Sorry, Hannah! Your grandma's the new main character!

HMM...

TK

TK

TK

Pi Phi's fall dance was tonight, but I didn't have a date or a costume, and I didn't want to drink, so.... I stayed home and drew. Niha didn't go, either, which made me feel better. I hope that everyone who went had fun!

Saturday, November 7

I woke up after NOON. I have to get on a regular sleep cycle this week...
HISSS
I DO NOT ANSWER TO THE SUN
Reading Astro City and Manhunter for superheroes class. Sooooo good!
My bedroom this year is tiny. 6'x9', to be precise. But we have 20' ceilings for some reason.....
6
No lie—
fleece jacket
+jeans
+Uggs
Every day is a variation
A-line coat
+dress
+boots
long shirt/sweater
+skinny jeans
+flats or boots
On one of these outfits!
I am treating it as an experiment in minimalism. I brought only clothes that are easy to match, so I can make the most outfits with the fewest items.
I like walking. I didn't used to— it felt lonely— but now it feels like a personal ritual.

Sunday, November 8

My cereal tastes rotten...
Now I have to find the time to march back there and get a refund... and cereal I can eat.
The expiration date says August 25!! Why did Safeway sell me cereal more than 2 months past its expiration date?! (puke face!)
Group project in the library: looking up children's periodicals from the Great War... and commenting on people who walk by.
He was cute.
Mm, but I envy you being a sophomore - with me, there's a 75% chance he's younger!
There's nothing wrong with dating a younger guy.
You're right. I just feel like an old perv anyway.
Walking to Safeway...
(molly)
Umm, the wagon story? A.K.A. that time I almost killed myself and Kelly?
It's sooooo funny!! Because you both lived!! Tell me the story again! Tell me again!
And back...
...I feel so dumb. The expiration date was August 25, 2010.
But the joke's on you, Safeway, because your cereal tastes like rot even when it's fresh, and I'm never buying it again.
You tell them.

Monday, November 9
I'm waking up a little bit earlier every day. My goal is up by 9, in bed by midnight.
Ooog...
The most evident
MOOOOOOOOOW!
MOOOOOOOOOW!
It's pouring again today. Biscuit keeps yowling to be let into his house... It breaks my heart!
I don't want to read about the Sunday School Movement anymooooore!!
Keep it together, girl!!
RESPONSIBLE SIDE
LAZY SIDE
Mow!
HISS!

Tuesday, November 10
WHAT. NO!
"STOP Air pollution" if you must deface a STOP sign!!
I was late to comics class for the first time, and on a day that we had a guest speaker!
ARG!
Who was I late for? That would be Marc Andreyko of Manhunter, A.K.A. Super Guest. He was insightful, funny, and seemed genuinely happy to be talking to our class. I waited in line after class to have my books signed and we talked some Death Note / Bakuman.
Last meeting for children's book class! Everyone's designs are beyond cute.

Wednesday, November 11

My only class today was canceled. I had all day to do my work, but only did half of it.

Hannah's birthday! Sushi, then drinks ♡

He brushed his teeth with deodorant!!!
We exchanged best stories about substance abuse (legal or other). Dylan's made me fall over laughing.
PFFF
No one stopped me...

Thursday, November 12
There is a foggy mountain in the distance. I see it when I walk home.
It pulls me in, until it feels like I could float over the houses and dissipate in that mist somewhere high and quiet.
But I can't go to that mountain.
I have to stay here and write papers
and make meals
and memorize kanji.

Friday. November 13

I only had one class today, and I skipped it to scan art in the library. That's some commitment to senioritis right there!

Script done for chapter one of my thesis comic!

Party at Lauren and Darcie's house!

I'm the turkey that lived.

GOBBLES!

Party at Dylan's house!
SALT!
SHOT!
LIME!
BURRO!
?

Saturday, November 14

I went out for groceries on foot, but I bought too much and killed my shoulders carrying it all home.

somehow, just eating an avacado made it feel better. I'm really growing to love them!

My parents bought 4 Duck football tickets for tonight, but it turned out that they couldn't make it to the game. As soon as I found girlfriends to go with, they called to say they'd promised them to my cousin.

SMACK

WOW

We went on a fun adventure to the stadium to pick up the tickets for my cousin, and I saw Autzen stadium lit up at night for the first time! Everything smelled like propane, and there were SO MANY PEOPLE!! I couldn't believe it!

I worked on my thesis and waited around for a call that never came.

Sunday, November 15

New study regiment: setting a 55 minute timer for tasks. Today went 55 min sakubun, 55 min Between Gears, 55 min freelance jobs, 55 min proofreading classmates' prospecti, 55 min thesis comic script, 55 min thesis paper, then freelance jobs and Between Gears again. I think it worked really well! I was surprised how much I could accomplish in less than an hour when I didn't take breaks.

Boom, boom, boom!
DONE!

BLEH

I never put on a bra today. My mother would be horrified. I even went out in public and rode a bike through campus!

Saw Pi Phis in the library!

Are you doing something new with your hair?
Uhh... Just not washing it...

I can't leave the house looking like this ever again!!!!!

Drew in the library until 2 AM.

Monday, November 16

I went to my Japanese professor's office at 11:05, only to find that the appointment was for 10:00. When she had a spare minute, I reached into my bag, only to find that I had packed the wrong essay.

ハリガットさん、大丈夫ですよ。みんな間違えますね。

I started crying uncontrollably! I was so frustrated with myself for messing up in so many ways so rapidly, and embarrassed for wasting my professor's time.

Amélie went to Panda express with me to cheer me up, but I realized that I had forgotten my wallet at home.

WORDS OF WISDOM FROM: AMÉLIE

Just bring champagne to my birthday...!

Everyone has days where it feels like they can't do anything right.

She baght me a Panda Bowl.

She really cheered me up.

Senior meeting potluck! It was so nice to see everyone again. I got the same question about 5 times:
Are those new glasses?
No... I don't wear them often, because I'm only mildly farsighted, but when I'm tired, my eyes need a little extra help.

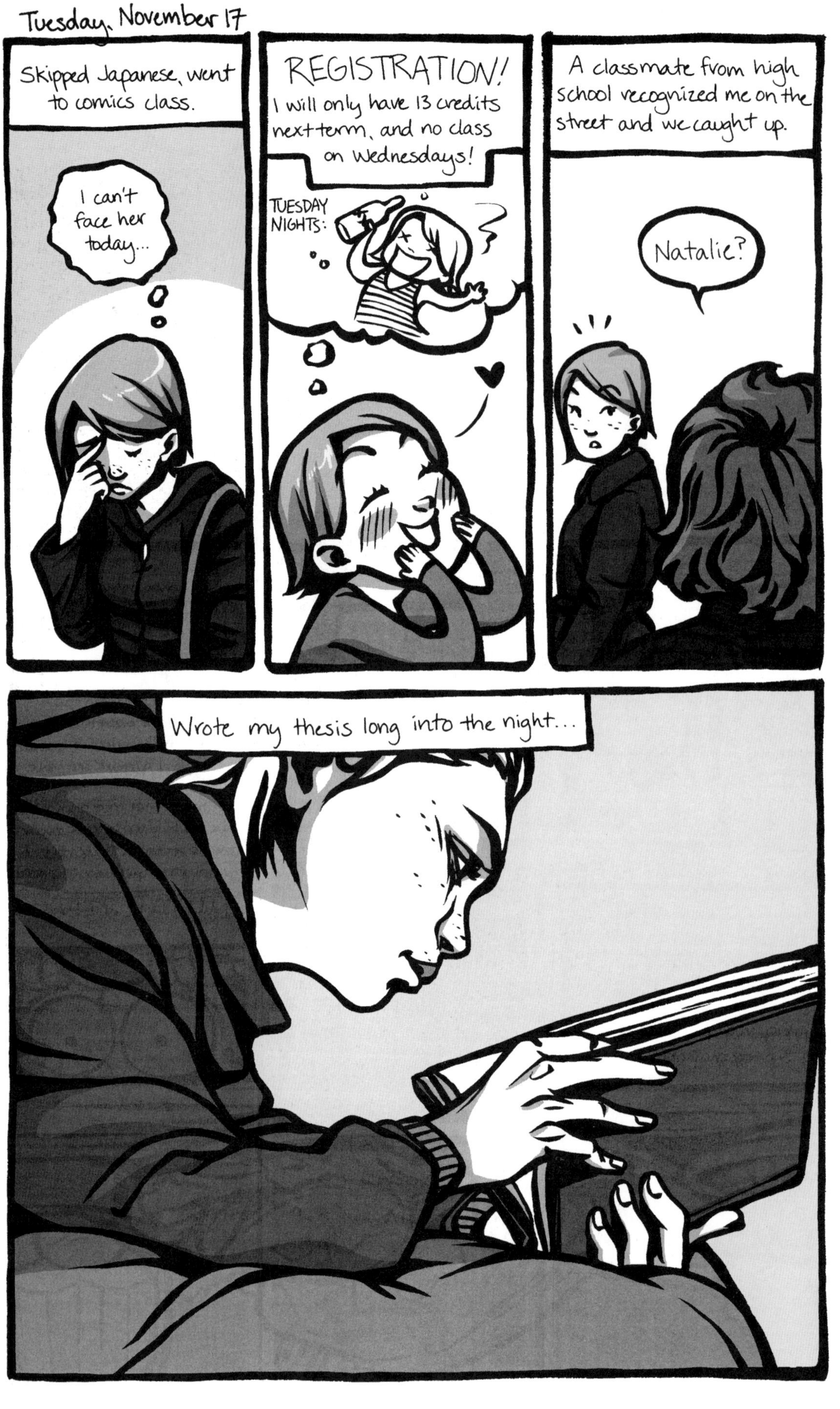

Tuesday, November 17

Skipped Japanese, went to comics class.
I can't face her today...

REGISTRATION!
I will only have 13 credits next term, and no class on Wednesdays!

TUESDAY NIGHTS:

A classmate from high school recognized me on the street and we caught up.

Natalie?

Wrote my thesis long into the night...

Wednesday, November 18

I dreamed that I lived in a world where Batman's villains were still around, but he had disappeared years ago. I had powers, but wasn't sure if I was ready to stand up to the villains yet.
I have to do some-thing!!
HELP!
It's so hard to get excited about showering when your house is 50°F.
BRR-BBBBR-BBR
JET recommendation letters from my high school Japanese teacher came today! THANK YOU!!!
habbuh?
Where does the time go?? I swear I don't waste it, but it's bedtime before I know what happened...

Thursday, November 19

I have been flatting color comic pages every day until my hand cramps.
>3<
♥
Kids, don't do this at home.

Ma'am? I'm gonna need you to let go there...

I sent my application for the JET Program today. Oh please oh please let everything be in order and let them clear me for the interview process!

Today in initiation, the senior class taught our dirty songs.
CENSORED
CENSORED CEN
Dance moves also censored

Friday, November 20

Went to the comic exhibit in the museum again, this time with Tyler. He knew all of the back stories for the characters, and I pointed out art techniques.
Went to the convenience store for a candy bar. I handed the cashier $1 in change, but he told me that it was only 85¢. I took back 2 dimes.
Alright, so that's 80¢...
... Right.
Nice try, sorority girl.
Got drinks with Tyler, Ty, Dylan, Alex, Ryan, and their friends.
People need to realize that feminism has a lot to offer men, too.
Oh, totally!
I love my guy friends.
I drunk dialed Jamie. I even tried to ask him serious questions about the comic industry for my thesis. *facepalm*
Tally...??
YEEEEP!!

Saturday, November 21

Initiatiownn!
There was freshly mown grass dumped in the alley randomly.
Mmm.... smells like soccer practice.

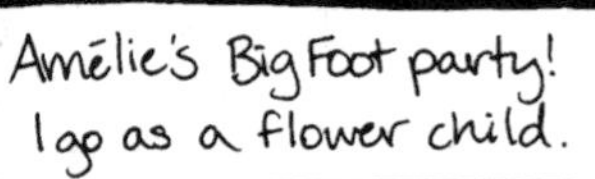
Amélie's Big Foot party! I go as a flower child.

Jello shots lead to bad decisions...
Hello??
...which I think is why boys bring jello shots to house parties.

Amélie let me pass out in her bed. Thanks, dude. Sorry for being ridiculous.

Sunday, November 22

Katie gave me a ride home and we laughed at everyone on the walk of shame.

My thesis prospectus is due tomorrow.

type type

writing...

type type type

writing...

writing...

DONE!

Weekly call home. ♡
さあ、おいで
Watched Sen to Chihiro no Kamikakushi.

Monday, November 23

Printed $20 of copies of my thesis prospectus for my class.
KTCH

Met Beth in Lillis to work on our evil group paper.
I promise I will be more into this class after my thesis prospectus is over.

I got pizza during a break in thesis prospectus class and got called out for eat-ing it in front of everybody like a tool.

Mmm, oh, wow. This smells soooo good, you guys!
just being facetious.....!!

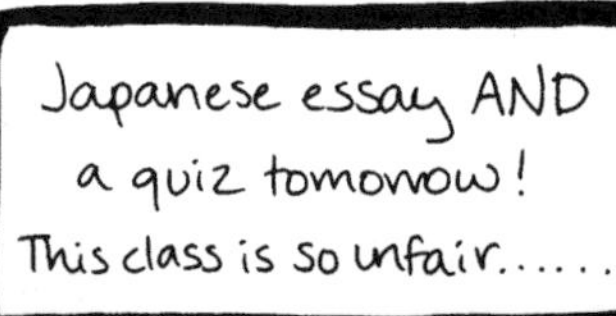

Japanese essay AND a quiz tomorrow! This class is so unfair......

Checked my tracking number and my JET application arrived on time!!!
YES!!

Tuesday, November 24

I think that I made a new friend in Japanese class! And we'll even have a class together next term!

Read The Boys after superheroes class.
Whaaaat the fuck.

Made 2 Christmas presents! Who could they be for...?

I went to the library at midnight and this adorable little raccoon cub crossed my path and looked up at me curiously.

I was about to kneel down and offer a hand, but caught myself just in time.
Oh. ohoho.
You almost got me!
?

Walking home, I looked up and saw the stars.
Oh.
WOW...

Wednesday, November 25

Z
Z
Z
Got up groggy and played Tetris for an HOUR! Hard time waking up today.

Packed and got out the door at 11:15 to meet Alex.
bump
Alex gave me a ride up to Portland. It was great catching up! We hit T-Bell for some face-stuffing goodness.
My love

Got home, hopped in the family van, and drove right back down I-5 for an hour on our way to Sunriver.
Whee.

Dad and I have been planning to make a sweet potato dish together for Thanksgiving, but it turns out that we had totally different recipes in mind!
With marsh-mallows.
No. With brown sugar.
Yeah, and marshmallows.
NO.

We watched The Mentalist on DVD as a family. I heart that show.
For the plot, huh?
Y-... Yeah...

Thursday, November 26
Dad, Nick, and Neil went skiing in the morning. I slept until noon!
I helped Mom get some dishes ready for Thanksgiving. Her sisters and Aunt Carol brought dishes and helped, but it's still so amazing to me that she keeps track of everything, from buying it to timing it just right.
I showed everyone my Wacom tablet and taught cousins Emily and Abby to draw with it.
Watched Zombieland with Nick and Neil. It was hilarious, but...
I COULDN'T SLEEP
I must have dreamed 20 different zombie scenarios, and woke up with pumping adrenaline and a cold sweat over and over again.
In the last dream, we were setting up legislation to prevent against future breakouts, and people were trying to cut corners in order to cut costs! I was like, hells no! It only takes one breach for this whole thing to happen all over again!

Friday, November 27

We skiid Bachelor today, but I am so out of shape that I needed a break in the middle of the climb to the base. :(
Tally? You okay?
GASP GASP
Not that difficult

NAP.

Drove into Bend with Mom on an errand.

Dad's 51st birthday!!!
Pecan pie! ♡

Dad recently spooled all of our old family videos onto DVDs. They are ADDICTING!!! I watched 1992-1996 in one sitting!!
LITTLE NEIL!!!!
Ooooh! That little voice!

Saturday, November 28

Drove from Sunriver to Portland with the fam.
Natural beauty of Central Oregon
Yawn.

Watched What Not to Wear with Mom. Whiskers was so affectionate!

KISS

PUR-R-R-R

Went to a party at Aunt Karin and Uncle Dave's condo, where we got to see Cousins Ryan and Steven, who live in So Cal.

They are very tall.

There was an E.coli scare in Portland. The news story flashed on the T.V. in the middle of the party.

Only person drinking water
3 glasses and counting

Went to New Moon with Ben, Molly, and Paul and teased it MERCILESSLY throughout.
HA HA HA!
Whisper
PFOOHOOHOOHOO!
psst
psst
...Which is the ONLY way anyone should watch those movies.

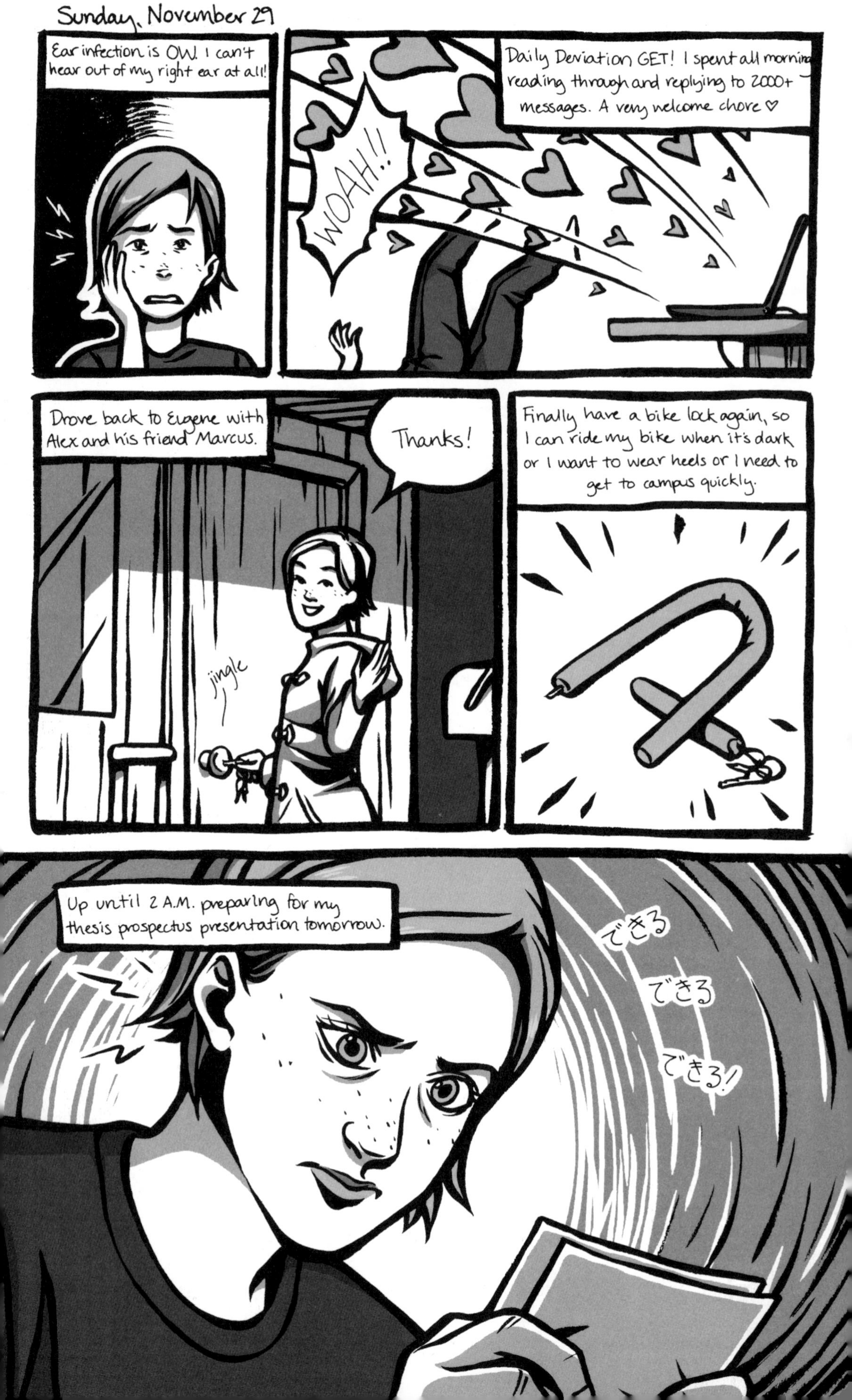

Sunday, November 29

Ear infection is OW. I can't hear out of my right ear at all!
Daily Deviation GET! I spent all morning reading through and replying to 2000+ messages. A very welcome chore ♡
WOAH!!
Drove back to Eugene with Alex and his friend Marcus.
Thanks!
jingle
Finally have a bike lock again, so I can ride my bike when it's dark or I want to wear heels or I need to get to campus quickly.
Up until 2 A.M. preparing for my thesis prospectus presentation tomorrow.
できる
できる
できる!

Monday, November 30

I wore heels for the first time in over a month. It hurts so good!

Thesis prospectus presentation! soooooooooooo nervous!!
So, ah, um,
like, such as
The Golden Age
like
Miyazaki
The Iraq
uhh...
sequential
Batman
Okay, it wasn't that bad. But I was so nervous that I started losing my voice and I can't remember it at all!

Ear infection is even worse today. I am not allowed to take Ibuprofen for the next 2 weeks because my tonsillectomy is approaching, but I NEEDED pain-killer, so I biked to Safeway for Tylenol. Every little bump made my ear THROB. It was like,

Quickly!!

...But gingerly.

...but quickly!!!

BUMP

Finished flatting a freelance project around 11 and just collapsed into bed.

Tuesday, December 1

Woke up at 5AM when the Tylenol wore off and my ear was SO PAINFUL. AAGH.
I didn't want to do anything besides go to the doctor's, but I studied for Japanese and emailed my teacher to be excused from class today.

At the health center....
I'm surprised that your eardrum hasn't burst yet . . .
NOOOOOO!!
At least I went in today and got some antibiotics. And she said that my tonsils are so big that they caused the infection, so it was a vote of confidence for my approaching tonsillectomy.

Didn't it say 'kanji quiz' on the schedule for today...? Since you came to class, I thought that meant you were prepared... that's the understanding.
I came because my doctor's appointment ended early and I didn't want to miss class if I didn't have to.
I can give you 80% if you take the quiz on Thursday.
Way to punish honesty. If I hadn't come today, I would have been excused from the quiz. Instead, I was punished for showing up after my appointment, wanting to catch the end of class. I can't believe I have to take 2 more terms of this.

She prescribed me amoxicillin and sudafed.
Oh! Exactly what I got!
And I'm, like, dizzy and no depth-perception.
F.M.L. today. Honestly.

Wednesday, December 2

Up again at 5:00 when the pain meds wore off.

The medications made me dizzy and reduced my depth perception, like the girl said. Writing is bizarre, and forget drawing.

d we actually found tha
n Britain and the US
etween children
Wobble
Presentation in Little Magazines class! Beth was cool and collected, but I was just trying to keep it together and not faint.

We're not going to have class together again, are we? I hope that we can be friends...

In the afternoon, my ear felt significantly better for the first time!
9740

In the shower, I noticed patches of red on my knees and back. They were hives. I'm allergic to amoxicillin.
ARE YOU JOKING?!
ARE YOU JOKING?!!

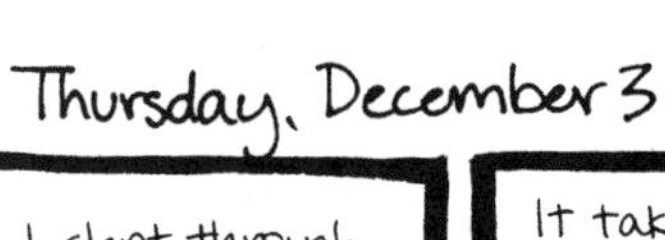
Thursday, December 3

I slept through the night! Feels so good...

It takes a lot to make me angry, but when I get to that point, LOOK OUT.
You asked for it,
you kept asking for it,
and today you're gonna get it.
Fact: women sometimes use their sexuality to intimidate other women.

Makin' Christmas presents!

Tyler called when he got off work and we went to his apartment to watch the football game, but we couldn't find it on basic cable! We went to Rennie's and miraculously caught the last 2 minutes!

I SMELL ROOOOOOOOSES!

Friday, December 4

LAST DAY OF CLASS!!
Pushy stalker classmate started asking for phone numbers. Noooo way. Not happening.
Avoid eye contact... wait until he's engaged in conversation with someone else...
slowly...
and...
BOLT!!

Got a new prescription antibiotic. And I officially have my second allergy: amoxicillin (and likely all penicillins). Damn.
Rx

Drew for HOURS uninterrupted for the first time all week!! My body doesn't hurt, I'm not breaking out in hives, Ducks are going to the Rose Bowl, school is OVERRR...

WOO!
It's time to......

CELEBRATE!!!!!!

Yeah, cuz you just can't keep me down

Oh, if you'd only give me

time

is really all that I need

to push it through

to make you see

I'll make you see!!

SPIN

SPINININ

SPIN

SPIN

NININ

I had a mini dance party in my room. Things got pretty wild.

Saturday, December 5
It's...... saturday?
So I don't have class....
And classes are over, so I don't have homework ......
I CAN DRAW
ALL
DAY!!
Sushi with the girls.
unbelievably soft and glossy!
Made friends with Alex at Hannah's house.
I LOVE YOU, ALEX.
Borrowed Blankets from Hannah.
Finally!
Text him!!
No, don't text him!!
I changed my vote to 'text him'.

Sunday, December 6
!
Woke up late! But I have so much to do today!! :(
Drew for hours.
Talked to Molly—she can drive me home for break!
That's great!!
By your logic, either I like you back or I'm the bad guy. Let me out of this box!
Tried to talk to my family while walking back from the grocery store. We couldn't hear each other and I got frustrated.
Went to the library and scanned art. I tried to find something I could use as a light box to trace through this really thick watercolor paper, but there was nothing like that there.
I guess I could use my window at sunrise...?

Monday, December 7
Bought Professor Freedman a little gift before our meeting as a thank-you for her help this term on my thesis.
Haircut! I went very short in the back. Yet again, my stylist gave me just the cut I wanted, but initially styled it in a frightening way (think Kate Goselin...). When I got home and played with it, I loved it.
Medical drama is back with a vengeance today. I ran out of Tylenol today and had to go out for more. I have a hard lump forming on my neck behind my ear, and the pain is back. Mom suggested microwaving a hand towel and holding it to my neck, but I only succeeded in setting my towel on fire. I have no hand towel and my ear hurts.
Group paper teammate took topics I was supposed to write about, wrote more than her share, and then was angry that I didn't write more.
I admire your work ethic, but you helped yourself, not the group.
1:00A.M.: Resumed Blankets, read deep into the night and finished.
Take me away, Craig.

Tuesday, December 8

Woke up at 9, called the doctor, and got an appointment 45min later.

Saw Professor Southworth in the library.
It seems like everyone is going to Sunriver for break! I was just talking to ____, and he's going.
REALLY?!

I have a different infection in the same ear, but at least I can start treating it.
Sigh

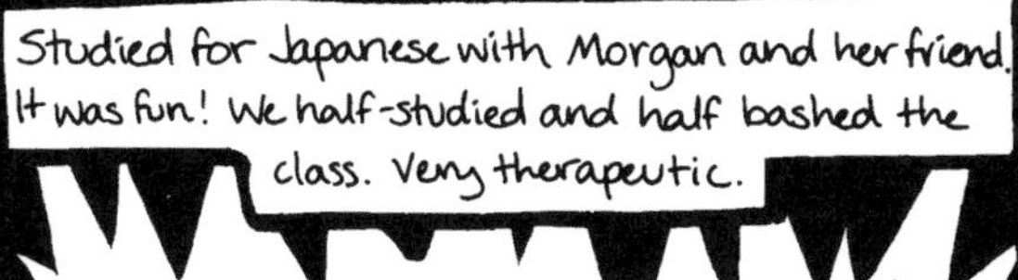

Studied for Japanese with Morgan and her friend. It was fun! We half-studied and half bashed the class. Very therapeutic.

Japanese final 6-8! I forgot 2 kanji compounds, gussed on 1 reading question, and otherwise felt comfortable. Come on, A-!

That Molly girl came again! We went to dinner, talked for hours, pretended to work, and had a sleepover!
Molly?
Yeah?
.....
Good night.
PFFFF!
HA HA HA HA...

Wednesday, December 9

I woke up before Molly and got a little inking in.
balancing shit on Molly

Worked through 2 weeks of dishes, but Molly kept me company and made it better.
Then what happened?
Well, it turns out that the narrator had been bitten by a zombie! And...

NANTS INGONYAMA BAGITHI BABA!!

Disney song rockout ♡♡ sess. on I-5. ♡♡

WO-
HOW DOES THIS KEEP GETTING BIGGER?!
-AH!!

I'm so happy to be home with my family for a few weeks.

How about this one?
There's a really full one over here.
I don't care.
They're all good.
I like this one.

We got a Christmas tree at a farm outside of town and then went to Outback Steakhouse.

Thursday, December 10

Went to Art Media for waterproof ink. I had a flirtation with a cute guy there last year, and I was curious to see if he was still there. He was! And not only that - he asked if I had gotten a haircut! He recognized me right away!

Doctor's appointment to make sure that all is well for the surgery tomorrow. It was, except that my doctor doesn't want me to go to Sunriver, as per the week-long family vacation we have planned. Secretly, we decide to do the surgery and go anyway. The danger is being too far from an emergency room for the next 2 weeks, but Bend has hospitals, too...

...
Let's just do it!

Decorated the Christmas tree!

Sketch group! I got to see Angie before her trip to China, give her and Emi their xmas presents, and Terry came, too! So fun!!

Mom called me home early, though, to take more fam photos.

But we took dozens before I left...!!

AUGH.

Friday, December 11

6:00AM check-in at the hospital.
Coffee?
Sorry, sweetie.
Stomach must be empty.

COOL TECHNOLOGY!!
SWIPE THERMOMETER
97°
SWIPE!
—WOAH!
HEATED GOWN!
PLASTIC I.V. Way less painful than metal!
VRRR
VRRRRR

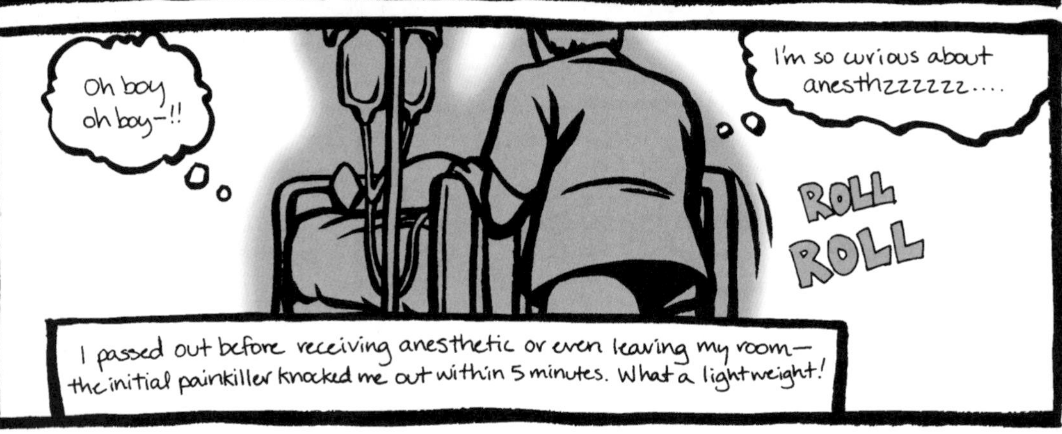
Oh boy oh boy—!!
I'm so curious about anesthzzzzzz....
ROLL
ROLL
I passed out before receiving anesthetic or even leaving my room—the initial painkiller knocked me out within 5 minutes. What a lightweight!

Tally? Dressed?
.... Tally??
PFZZZZZZ
Woke up back in my room, but couldn't stay awake for more than 5 minutes. Kept passing out in the funniest places... clothes half on, tying my shoes, waiting for the wheelchair with my head on the wall, in the wheelchair, in the car trying not to puke on the way home...

You know... You do have an anti-nausea suppository...
NO!
Oh pride.

Slept most of the day. Anything involving focusing my eyes made me nauseous, so no reading or art.
K.O.

Saturday, December 12
Still sleepy, no trouble falling asleep in any position/light.
BLAR
Swallowing hurts like hell. I'm still nauseous, but able to get down some scrambled eggs and coffee.
cough!
drip
drip
Felt extremely accomplished when I sent out an Etsy order. I typed up the thank you letter, addressed the envelope, and cut out cardboard reinforcements all by myself!
Yes!
Extra weak, slow fist pump
Finished inking the Catwoman commission! Let's pump out the art while I feel alright!
Played card games with Mom and Dad.
...for 18.
...14, Sweetie.
Please stay for a few more games. Your mother and I have had low cribbage self-esteem...

Sunday, December 13

Woke up late, hadn't had pain meds since midnight, felt AWFUL.
!

I couldn't eat. Even trying to drink water, it came out of my nose!

Kept asking Mom when I could take my next dose of Oxycontin.
2 more hours.
hnnn
1 more hour.
HNNN!!

I understand the appeal of popsicles now.

Molly came over. We watched The Soup and family videos. I tried to explain some Norwegian xmas tree decorations to her in Oxycontin speak.
It has, like... subtle... colors.
And swirly.
Flumes. 'S pretty.
— whee!

Monday, December 14

I felt sooooo sick that I took the suppository anti-nausea medicine.
• • • • • •
Goodbye, butt virginity.

That medicine intensified the effects of the pain killer, which just knocked me out. I fell asleep EVERYWHERE. I'm like a frickin' cat on these drugs!
ZZZZZ
!

XSZZ...
Hardwood floor!!

IS THIS NORMAL?!
MFZZZ... MFZZ...

Tuesday, December 15

When I drink things, they come out my nose. Is my throat healing correctly?!!
OW OW OW!
medicines BURN

According to the internet, yes. It seems to be a common problem.
Okay...

EWWW
My hairstyle is starting to bother me. Why does it poof in the back?!

I ventured outside today to give an art lesson to the Jesuit HS Japanese club. Memories~♥ Japanese club meant a lot to me in high school; I was in the club all 4 years, was president for one year, and went to Japan to do a homestay with a group from Japanese club. It was great to visit again.

A bunch of people came up at the end of club to show me their artwork. Everyone was so talented... I hope that they find the same joy from art after high school that I did.
I have witnesses.
I mean, if you want, I can come again in the spring...
Yes please!
Yeah!
Um, YEAH.
On top of it all, Sensei sent me home with cookies she baked and a $20 Kinokuniya gift certificate!

Wednesday, December 16

I've lost 5 lb.s in less than a week! I won't lie—I'm a little bit happy about it, but I don't want to get thinner at the expense of my health... ribs = yuckers.

It's because of the tonsillectomy pain meds... I can't stomach much food...

Went to Starbucks to deliver a commission!

The family gathered to watch the first half of UP tonight. I tried so hard not to cry, but who am I kidding? EVERY TIME.

More super-secret drawin' times for the holidays!
Censored!

Thursday, December 17

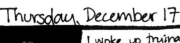

I woke up trying to eat my pillow. I thought it was a donut and I wanted the frosting.

?

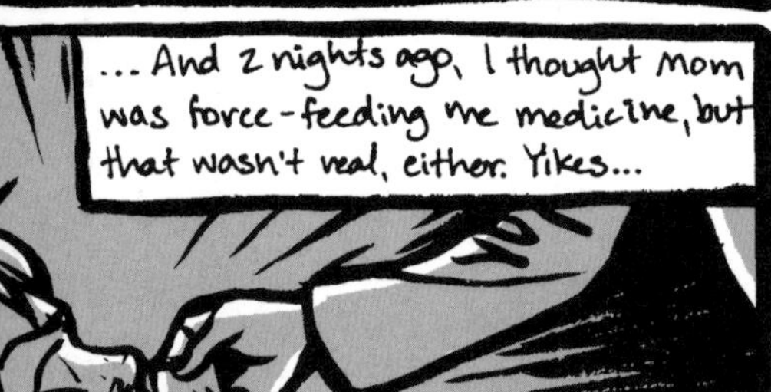
I also thought I heard our car being broken into, and actually went outside to check on it, worrying my family.
?

...And 2 nights ago, I thought Mom was force-feeding me medicine, but that wasn't real, either. Yikes...

We made peanut butter balls tonight— a Nourigat tradition! 1 part butter, 2 parts peanut butter, and 3 parts powdered sugar mixed and formed into small spheres, then frozen overnight, dipped in chocolate, and frozen again. Sohohoho good!!

It's funny, but no matter what time of year it is, it doesn't feel like Christmas until we do these annual rituals like making PBBs, signing xmas cards, and decorating the tree.
Isn't that the truth? Be careful what you start with your family—your kids will come to expect whatever rituals you start!

You know this is a popular street drug? People want this effect.
But I can feel it making me ill...!
It's because most people are so miserable, they want to feel numb.

Terry came over to keep me company!
I come bearing gifts!
flap
flap
We watched Summer Heights High and he left me with some homework to do in Sunriver next week (Buffy Season 1, Bone Vol 2, Lost At Sea, Vogue Sep Iss.).

Friday, December 18
Come on, Sweetie
Mom woke me up at 10 to get ready for our trip to Sunriver.
I feel awful today for some reason. I can't finish my breakfast.
WORDS OF WISDOM FROM: NICK
So is our last name Norwegian?
Actually, I'm pretty sure our last name's French. But I don't give a crap about that stuff. I'm from America and I speak American. People only care about heritage because they want to belong to a club.
Amused
I slept for most of the 5hr drive.
Wearing a coat backwards to block light
We stopped in Redmond to look at a Subaru Outback we are hoping will replace the family car that I learned to drive on: our '95 Volvo 960. I kept sleeping.
SUBARU
We got to Sunriver at 6:30. I hugged my my aunt and uncle and went straight to bed.

Saturday, December 19

We went into Bend around dinnertime with Aunt Karin and Uncle Dave for the Sons of Norway Lodge's christmas pageant.

My grandma is a religious member of Sons of Norway, and she organized a lot of the show. She played piano for many of the songs.

This year, she asked if I would play Saint Lucia, since they didn't have a girl quite the right age. Traditionally it would be a teenager, but I look like I'm 16 anyway, right? I was happy to be able to do something for her.

sounds kind of fun...!
(November hair)

I walked around the room in two slow circles, holding a tray of cookies and leading the younger children, who then took the cookies and passed them out to the adults. The hardest part was keeping my head still and not lighting myself on fire!

I think your grandpa lost a button right here.
You make a beautiful Lucia!
I was thrilled to make my family happy, even if all I did was walk in a circle.

Sunday, December 20

We had an early Christmas celebration today with my mom's family. I was still really sick, and only came out for about an hour, but it was fun to see everyone.

We have 4* December birthdays in the fam, so we also exchanged gifts for that.
Me
Aunt Gwen
Cousin Emily

*1 for cousin Steven in CA

I had an embarrassment of riches by the end!

My cousins Abby and Emily made me comics. How precious is that??
Nick got me Parks & Recreation season 1, and we spent the afternoon watching it.
GLOMP!
heel kick of approval
YOU DID GOOD.

I was only able to eat half of my coffee, a few sips of apple juice, and a popsicle today.

I should...
eat tomorrow...

Monday, December 21

I'm back up to 2 tsp of pain killer per dose. It makes all the difference. Today, I was able to eat a full breakfast and lunch and leave the house to shop with Mom.
BOUNCE

Winter Solstice! Shortest day of the year!

MOW.
MOW.
Oh, oxycontin time?

I have transcended language.
Purrrrr

"Life needs secret plans," and I have a few. I have no idea how I'm going to make this one happen, though.

Bleaching my hair! Panic and excitement and freaky, freaky orange hair.

Tuesday, December 22

It's my golden b-day!! I love my birthday— it's the first day that starts getting longer after the solstice.

Note: born at 4AM

My hair is crazy, but I think it's just because I haven't used the blonde dye yet.

super damaged

I am wrong. It's still crazy after dying and deep conditioning. Just way too brassy and light for my face. Yikes. Mom helped me with every step and even paid for some of the products I used, and I feel like I wasted her good will on a horrible decision.

better I guess?

Well, heh, it's appropriate for my "Golden" birthday.
I like it, Honey! It's bold!

You're beautiful— not just because you're my daughter; you truly are.
Thanks, Dad.

I WON AT SORRY!!

I got an iPod nano with video recording from Mom and Dad! AW YEAH!! I've had the same original mini since 2004, but its battery has been dead for years, it doesn't sync with iTunes, and I only use it in its iHome dock anymore. But NO MOOOOORE!!!

OMIGOD OMIGOD OMIGOD OMIGOD

OMIGOOOOOOOOOOOOOOOOOOD!!

Wednesday, December 23

We packed up early and were on the road home by 9:00. I drove with Dad in the new Subaru.
It was fun just talking with Dad for 3 hours. I think the quality of conversations gets better the longer you're alone with someone.

I made an appointment downtown to fix the hair, and tried to meet people while I was out. I swung by Periscope, said 'hi' to everyone, and dropped off a little comic I made about the studio. Jeff Parker gave me his Exiles trade, Point of No Return, unknowingly fitting the caricature from my comic! You're just too nice, Parker!

In case your school doesn't assign enough reading.
Thank you!!!

I also saw Jamie in a cafe next to the salon, and gave him his xmas present and bugged him in the middle of writing.

Hi Jamie! Ooh—
What's that?
What's that?

Hair: you could say it's fixed!

still extremely light blonde, but a color more likely to be found in nature.

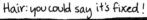

JAMMIES!

Mary and Molly came over, and we imitated the SNL skit by having a pajama party and pretending to play with knives.

Thursday, December 24

Present wrappin'!

Nourigat family tradition: the only gift we open on Christmas Eve is from Mom+Dad, and it's always pajamas.
PLUS a robe and slippers this year!! THANK YOU♡!!

Dad's family came over for Christmas dinner. I re-met my cousin Zack, and little cousin Chase turned our 17-year old cat Whiskers into a kitten again with just a piece of string.
Who knew he could still play like that...?

I waited until Mom and Dad were asleep, snuck downstairs, and grabbed the family photo albums for reference for their Christmas paintings.

I stayed up until 4:30 working, but I couldn't finish Mom's gift.
Christmas fail.

Friday, December 25

Nick and Neil came in to wake me up at 7. They got to see a side of their big sister that they never had before.
HISS

THE GREAT STAIR RACE

I got panties in my stocking....?

Mom, these are really cute!

Oh yeah, those are!

...Are you seeing these for the first time...?!

...Oh my God-Dad was in Victoria's Secret BUYING ME UNDERWEAR?!!

EDIT: No, he wasn't. Mom was just playing along.

Santa brought me a glorious, glorious 11"x17" scanner. Oh boy oh!!!

This is the best box I've gotten on Christmas since I was, like, 6.
REC

It was a great year for Miyazaki: Ponyo, Totoro art book, and Starting Point. My favorite presents were probably those plus UP, Never Learn Anything from History, the scanner of course, and Paris Je T'aime.

Book + DVD person

Mom, Dad, and I watched Paris Je T'aime. They initially were only in for 2 shorts, but they stayed for over an hour. Suuuuuch a good movie. I cried uncontrollably for Place des Victoires, like I always do, and Place des Fêtes, which I never had before.

Saturday, December 26

I feel ill... I've had problems with blood pressure and head-aches the last 2 days. Very strange....
Oh...
wooo...

Helped clean the house for Mom and Dad's party tonight.

I want kids, but I don't want them to get in the way of my other goals.
What would you do if you didn't have kids??

...
Oh, right. You'd find plenty to do, wouldn't you?

First time driving since surgery! (I am Oxycontin free!) Dad gave me the keys to the Lexus and I didn't crash it.
Thank God!

Fell asleep at 7:00.
THIS IS ALL I DO ANYMORE.

Sunday, December 27
I got Phoenix's Wolfgang Amadeus for xmas, and I'm listening to 1901 on repeat. Pretty wonderful beat.
FALLIN FALLIN FALLIN FALLIN
FALLIN
FALLIN FALLIN
Mom made me go on a walk with her around our neighborhood. I thought it was going to kill me, but she knew best (of course), and I felt much better the rest of the day.
COUGH COUGH WHEEZE
It's my BIRTHDAY!!!!! NW Portland bar hop~!!
It was a mix of high school, college, and comics friends, but I think that people got along. I think they're all great, so hopefully they thought the same of each eachother.
How I got out of doing karaoke:
Oh... I can't... Y-you know, my tonsils...
PSHH. WHATEVER!
Emiii! Don't go alone!!
Damn, she can run! I thought she was going to give up after a block!
Don't worry, I'll get her.
DASH

Monday, December 28

Rough morning... I woke up at 7, 8, 10, and finally got up at 11. I've never thrown up from alcohol, but this morning felt like maybe that would have been better than holding it in and feeling nauseous...

I went to Periscope in the afternoon, and drove the new car for the first time! I'm listening to Atmosphere's When Life Gives You Lemons.
♪ You love the people that love you ♪

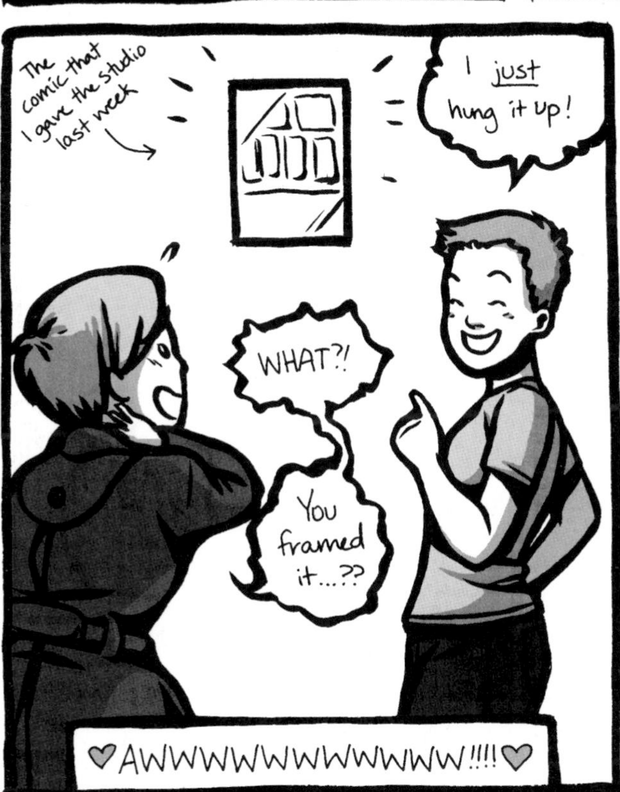
The comic that I gave the studio last week
I just hung it up!
WHAT?!
You framed it...??
♥AWWWWWWWWWWWW!!!!♥

Okay. To be a serial killer, you must kill 3 strangers over at least 1 month and have some sort of common method...
The Emitown Slasher? Does that sound good?
Why are we thinking about this so much?!
Ha ha ha ha!
Emi contemplates her serial killer alter-ego.

Ha ha ha ha!
Ha Ha ha! ha!
I love this place.

Tuesday, December 29

SNOW WATCH '09:
Oh, SHIT!
FIRST SIGHTING!

'Played' in the snow with Cat and Ron!
SLIP!
SKID
SLIP!

Emi came and we got sushi!
I need pics of you for my phone's photo I.D.!
Oh, I want your pics, too!
Me, too!
CLICK!
CLICK!
CLICK!

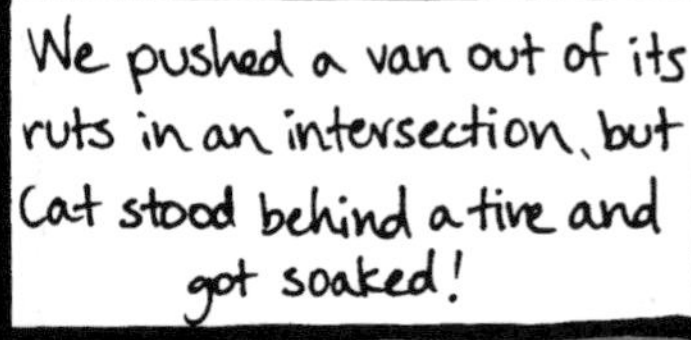
We pushed a van out of its ruts in an intersection, but Cat stood behind a tire and got soaked!

No good deed goes unpunished!

PEPPERMINT PATTIES!
DIVE-TASTIC

Wednesday, December 30

Went downtown early with Dad and got coffee before heading to Periscope.

Laura Hudson from Comics Alliance came into the studio. That lady is rad! We talked about Astro City, Gotham Central, and Batwoman (thank you, superheroes class, for the reading list!).

Met Mom and Dad for dinner at Higgins in SW. Had the most amazing salmon steak I have EVER eaten.

Mom took me to see Beauty & The Beast at the Newmark Theatre. It was delightful!

Mom told me, "I took you to see Beauty & The Beast when it came out. You were about 4, and when Beast was dying, you looked up at me, with tears streaming down your face, as if to say—"
That can happen?

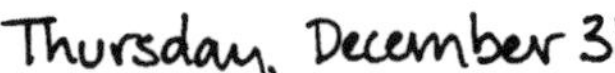
Thursday, December 31

Terry and Joëlle came into Periscope to drop off some pages and take me out to lunch!! (Yes, I was just at Sushi Station. What are you trying to say?!) I do so like those two♡

Ahhh-some New Years house party at Steve Lieber and Sara Ryan's!

DRAMA
LLAMA
I was not made for drama. It makes me want to run away.
MAA

I've decided not to date anyone in comics again.
I feel like it's the equivalent of dating in the office... it's wonderful when things work out, but if they don't, the breakup is ten times as destructive.

Friday, January 1

Mom and I went to a matinee showing of The Princess And The Frog. I almost cried at SEVERAL parts of the movie. (What is happening to me??) Great movie. Loved the two main characters. ♡
sniff!
AGAIN?!!
ROSE BOWL
Ducks lost, but at least we GOT THERE! First time in 15 years!
FAN
1
I can pretend for a day!
Went to Emily's birthday party for a short while, met her boyfriend, and gave her Twilight fanart. She gave me a 'locker cling' of Troy Bolton! KYAAAA!!
Ack! Under-dressed!
2010 GOALS!
1 Make a GREAT thesis
2 Graduate
3 Have fun and sell stuff at ECCC and Stumptown
4 Finish Between Gears
5 Start my next big comic
6 Get a JOB!

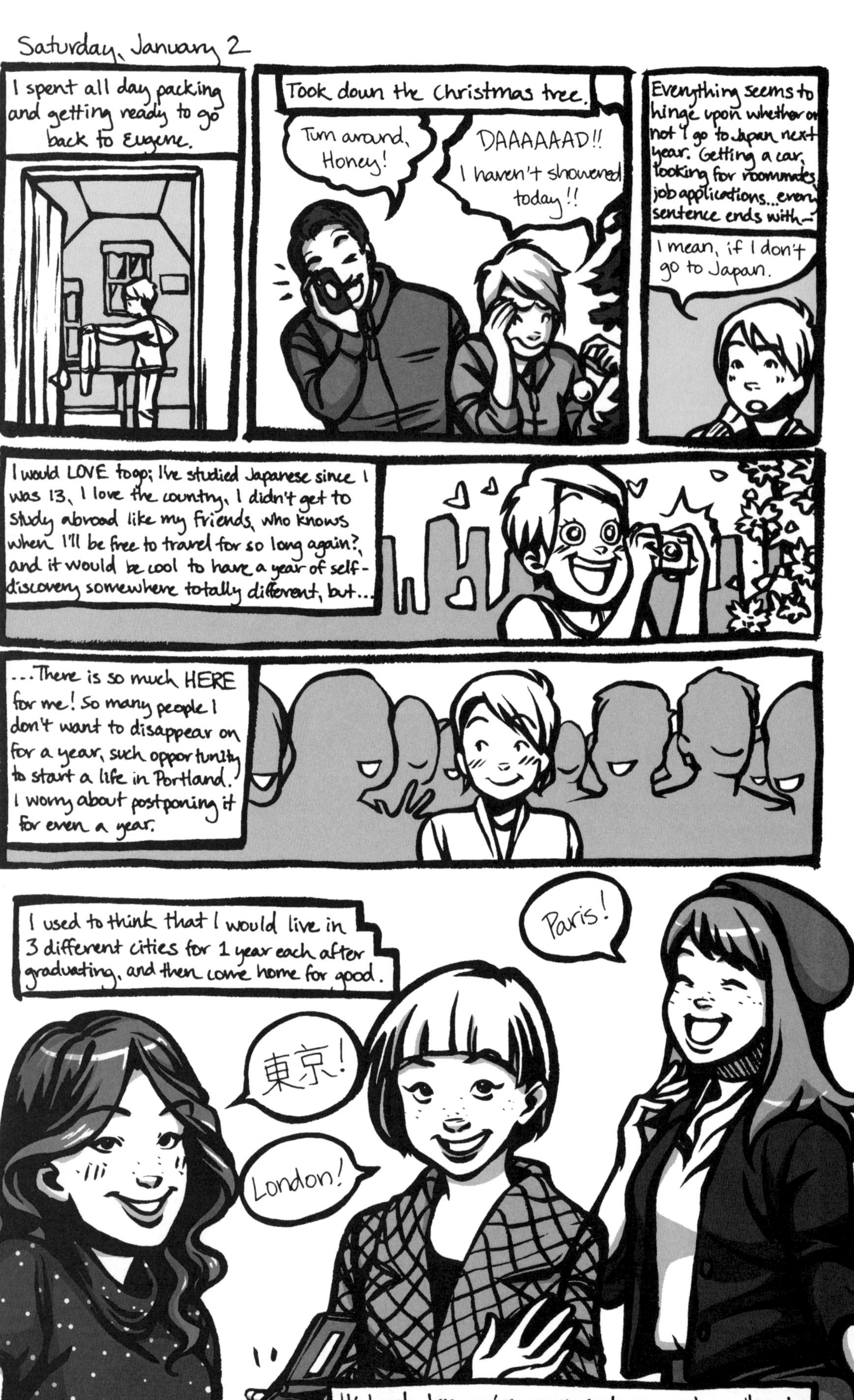
Saturday, January 2
I spent all day packing and getting ready to go back to Eugene.
Took down the Christmas tree.
Turn around, Honey!
DAAAAAAD!! I haven't showered today!!
Everything seems to hinge upon whether or not I go to Japan next year. Getting a car, looking for roommates, job applications... every sentence ends with—
I mean, if I don't go to Japan.
I would LOVE to go; I've studied Japanese since I was 13, I love the country, I didn't get to study abroad like my friends, who knows when I'll be free to travel for so long again?, and it would be cool to have a year of self-discovery somewhere totally different, but...
...There is so much HERE for me! So many people I don't want to disappear on for a year, such opportunity to start a life in Portland. I worry about postponing it for even a year.
I used to think that I would live in 3 different cities for 1 year each after graduating, and then come home for good.
Paris!
東京!
London!
It's hard when you've grown roots somewhere, though.

Sunday, January 3

Moved back to Eugene. Mom helped me set up the new scan station.
Aw yeah. That's nice.
Mom took me grocery shopping and paid for it (whoo hoo!!)! She offered to help me move all of my stuff upstairs, but she had done plenty for me and I sent her home.
WORDS OF WISDOM
FROM: THOMAS JEFFERSON
Never trouble another for what you can do for yourself.
I went shopping for course books and listened to MUSIC, while WALKING, on the new iPod !!!!!!!! GAH, it's a whole new world when I walk....!
I'm back in my stupid little room, in my stupid little bed with my feet poking out over the edge and hitting my studid little desk... but I slept so well!
Burrito Technique

WINTER

Monday, January 4

No class until 7pm!! Bring on the arttttttt.

7-10pm class is a film class on Kiyoshi Kurasawa. I signed up expecting samurai movies, but alas, they are horror. First names can make a big difference...

shudder

TUG

I went to the library to look for biplane reference and found an entire aisle on aviation!!
♡!
I repeat: I see something new and magical every time I go to the library!

I lost so much weight after the surgery that my period didn't come this month!
Don't die, Uterus!!
I need to gain some weight...

And so...
SMACK!
Raw cookie dough

Tuesday, January 5

12AM: Women and Gender Studies: Women in Literature, Art, and Society. Our first readings are A Room of One's Own and Mrs. Dalloway!

EEEEE EEEEE EEEEE

2PM: JPN 415: Written Japanese. Last term was so bad that I considered changing my language-intensive major to culture-intensive *just* to avoid this teacher. I gave her written feedback with several specific suggestions for the class, and today I found out that she is instituting changes this term... that are exactly the opposite of my suggestions. Really?

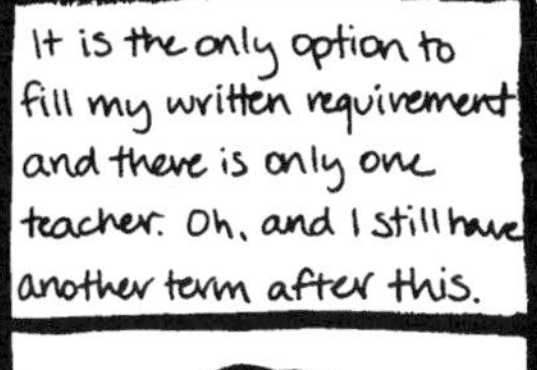

It is the only option to fill my written requirement and there is only one teacher. Oh, and I still have another term after this.

I... I cannot take 22 more weeks of her...

Is it still possible to change to culture-intensive?
My Japanese major adviser ♡
YES.

Is it wrong to change to culture-intensive?
Professor I trust ♡
NO.

Do you care if I change to culture-intensive?
Mom ♡
NO.

...

OKAY!

I am now a culture-intensive Japanese major. That means I need 4 upper-level culture courses to graduate, and no more language.

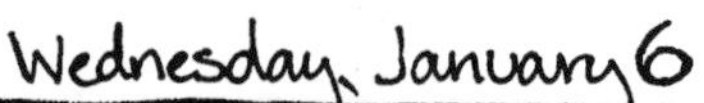
Wednesday, January 6

First Wednesday of the term! My goal for Wednesdays is to work on my thesis ALL DAY, since I have no classes. Today it went pretty well. I woke up and did thumbnails...

...Went to the gym, showered, and took thumbnails to Starbucks to work on...

I forgot how AMAZING working out makes your skin look!!

And how it magically cures sore artist back!!

...Bought groceries, came home, and finished the thumbnails. A lot of other chores made their way in, but I did a lot of good work, too!

YEAH

GNAW GNAW

FEELIN' THE GROOVE

There were so many cute guys in the grocery store today. MAN. Why am I so busy? And why is there no way to start up a conversation in a grocery store?!
So, you like grapes?
Uhh...
I LOVE grapes.
...
N—
'SUP
We should get together some time and eat grapes. Lemme give you my #...

DAFFODIL SHOOTS!

I LOVE daffodils. In the darkest, coldest months of winter, when all hope of spring has faded, they push through the icy ground to say, "The end is near! Beauty and warmth are on the way, and we will tide you over until they get here."

Thursday, January 7

I talked to my women and gender studies class today about my A Room of One's Own comic. It was really flattering, but I was so embarrassed... I haven't studied this subject as much as a lot of my classmates have, and I don't want to come off as ignorant.

I feel like things are a lot better than they were in 1928...?

I mean, about half of my creative mentors are male...?

And I don't feel like there's much hostility toward women in creative professions...??

Caffeine headache! I often put my coffee behind my curtain (next to my desk), and sometimes I forget that it's there and I don't drink it before leaving the house.

6PM: (New class!) Japanese Literature 1600-1868. Attack of the high kid!!

Do you think that old guys having sex with little kids back then is why Japanese men are so effeminate today?

...

WTF NO HIGH KID.

Friday, January 8
No class today, either! I've been going pedal-to-the-metal since coming to college, and the free time this term is bewildering.
What should I even do?
DRUM
DRUM
AHA HA!
I put on a pair of knee socks I got in my stocking, only to find that they are OVER-the-knee-socks!!
Gasp! Santa!!
Dana, Amy, and Kira's Splash of Color party!
Black dress + black shoes + BLUE stripe
Black shirt + Black pants + RED belt
white shirt + black skirt + RED purse
Bars with Hannah and Danielle—
NGG SOWA WEAM
OOOOMIGOOOMMMM
—followed by the taco cart.

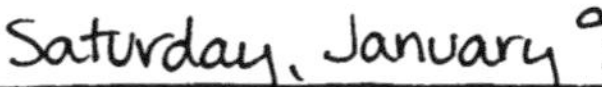
Saturday, January 9

Went to The Princess and the Frog with Kayla. We went to Starbucks first and snuck our coffee into the theater!
I put a stopper in the top and hold it upright in my purse like this.
I see!
Ha ha, I feel like I'm teaching you how to steal....!

Easy~~ Easy~~!!
I inked the first page of my thesis comic today. It was terrifying to set pen irreversibly to paper, but I'm glad I got it out of my system now.

Glass of wine and Dollhouse catch-up!!
OMIGOD, OMIGOD, OH-OMIIGOD
Sooooo much love. This season is amazing. I want to draw fan art for every episode.

Sunday, January 10

There's so, so, SO much art to do. (But I was very productive today!)

Eep.

Dad helped me edit my resume and talked me through the job search. He knows exactly how to phrase things!

You literally call him or her up and say, '(insert impossibly smooth pitch here)'
Wow!

I would hire me if I spoke like that. Unfortunately, I do not. I have much to learn and I think I am going to have to try pretty hard to land a good job.

Watched the latest Dollhouse episode, 'Getting Closer.'

WWWWHHYYYYYYYY?!!!!!
YOU WERE MY FAVORITE!!!
SOB

It's killing time (and worse!) in Whedon-land. It's a testament to the show that I care this much about the characters, though.

Monday, January 11

BANG

I think that the hardest part of living with me is that I am a light sleeper and I HATE being woken up. Thick walls make good room-mates, but our house this year is cheap and thin.

Stumptown registration opened today! Overly-eager, I filled out an application for a half table and stuck it in the mail, just like last year, forgetting that Angie, Emi, and I had talked about sharing a table.

DUMB.

I suck. Hopefully we can fix my mistake!

I met Darcie for coffee and shot the breeze with her. That lady is hilarious! I'm excited to hear about her plans to start a webcomic and become an international spy (shhh).

This week's Kurosawa film: Charisma.
What the fuck.
What the fuck.
What the fuck.
What the fuck
What the fuck
What the fuck
(I actually ended up really liking it, though! Ha ha.)

Tuesday, January 12

New alley cat.
I shall call you Minerva!!

GROW - OUT
What now...?
Options are:
A) Get a super-short haircut
B) Blend blonde highlights into the dark roots
C) Dye hair back to its natural color

I'm already excited about tomorrow!
Thesis Day Thesis Day drawing in a cafe Thesis Day ♪

twiddle

VAAAAAAAAAAST stretches of free time. I went to class, did all of my homework for the week, worked on all of my current art projects, read a comic, watched 3 T.V. shows, and still had time left. WHAT.

Wednesday, January 13
Oh, that rain on a tin roof sound...
pit pit pit pit pit pit pit pit pit
Thesis Day! I went to Starbucks to draw, but it was raining for the entire walk there.
Don't you dare ruin my art boards, rain!!!!!!!
I played a 48-song Disney sing-along playlist.
I wanna walk like you ♫ talk like you, too-oo-oo!! ♪
I'm the best kind of immature, I swear.
So we'll do a set of 5, then 10, 15, 20, 25, and back down 20, 15, 10, and 5. Ready?
NOD
...
Hannah and Dana took me to the gym and dragged me through their ab workout. Ouch! I need that kind of tough love to get to the gym regularly, though.

Thursday, January 14

!
Oh MAN...
My abs.
My shoulders.
My back.
I'll be in such good shape when Hannah and Dana are done.

I hope to one day be wealthy enough to afford regular massages. This is a real goal of mine. It relieves the tension that causes my 'Sore Artist Back'.

As far as I can tell, the worst knots (in my shoulders and upper back) are caused by holding my arms steady over my desk as I draw.

On a whim, I hiked the Hendricks Park area. It was wonderful! I communed with nature, as they say.

Now my body REALLY hurts!
THROB
THROB
THROB
THROB

Friday, January 15

No class Friday! I worked on the Between Gears minicomic cover, my thesis, and a freelance project. Boy howdy, life is good right now!

Now everything REALLY REALLY hurts. That must have been quite the workout yesterday.

Ow.

Ow.

I didn't leave the house at all today. If I'm aware that I'm a loser, does that make it better?

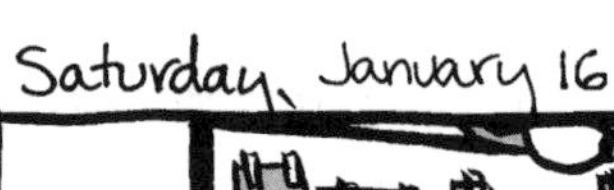
Saturday, January 16

Niha went home for the weekend and I had some karaoke time in the empty house.
Or somebody else may tell me, and whisper the words just right

Darcie's birthday party!! The theme was 'school carnival,' and we played some AMAZING games like... PRETTY KITTY

Are you my pretty kitty?
POKE
HA
HA
Meow!

Blindfold 1 person and sit 3 people in a row of chairs, side-by-side. Give the blindfolded person 2 wooden spoons, which they can use to 'feel' the 3 people and try to identify them. They can also ask, "Are you my pretty kitty?" And whoever they ask has to reply, "Meow!"

NECKING!

snk!

Pass an orange around in a circle, person to person, using only your necks. Every time someone drops the orange, they are out and the circle gets smaller until there is only one person left!

FISHING!

I got a dinosaur!

Ring Pop!

Novelty miniature condom...?

Hang a curtain over the bottom half of a doorframe and put someone on the other side with a bunch of prizes. Line up one-by-one and drop a 'line' with a clothespin 'hook' over the curtain. When you feel a tug, pull up your prize!

I feel safe from here on — you don't have to walk me all the way.
No, I insist! I wouldn't feel right if I didn't.
8D ♡

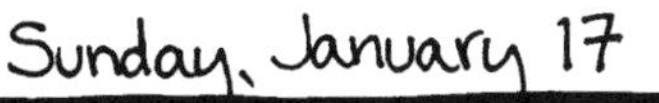
Sunday, January 17

I put on the jeans I wore last night. Contents of my back pocket:
BOTTLECAP
STICKY NOTE THAT READS 'DUMBLEDORE'
DUMBLEDORE
PLASTIC DINOSAUR
EPIIIIIIIIIIIC.

UGH, unlaze, body! Please!!
Wake up! We have SO MUCH WORK TO DO!!
(Poor Responsible side. No one listens to her.)

Suddenly, I have a reason to care what my house looks like.

DISHES DONE

LAUNDRY GOING

TEE HEE HEE!!

FLOOR SWEPT

RUMBA RUMBA

Monday, January 18
Every day, I am thankful for my new scanner. It has seriously changed my life not having to carry my originals to campus and wait for the only 11"x17" scan station to open up every time I want something scanned.
Reorganized the living room furniture, which flushed out a few spiders, including a massive brown recluse. Noooooooooooo.
Please don't have a family...!!
SLAP
Tyler gave me his extra T.V. in exchange for a drawing of Spider-Woman. Movie-viewing capabilities GET!
Ha ha ha!!
Went to Where the Wild Things Are with Nathan.

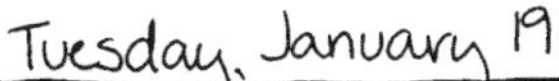

Tuesday, January 19

I've had a migraine aura* for the past several days. I've been careful about avoiding certain lights that trigger them for me, but you can never be sure what will trigger one...
Pleeeease don't turn into a migraine...
*Altered consciousness that warns me I have a migraine coming on... like that feeling you get before a thunderstorm.

Watched It's Always Sunny in Philadelphia on the new T.V. setup.
Nice.
This one has been on my list for a while!
My comics came back to me safely, and I have House of M to read now!

My Japanese Lit. class enjoys the comments of High Kid.
WTF High Kid?!?
(Gordon's nickname for him is 'Permahigh'!)

Wednesday, January 20

STRETCH

Thesis Day! Late start, but I am still well on track for my thesis comic.

Yyyyawn

This is good! I think we have achieved a second date...!

tap

tap tap

Finished page 4 of the thesis comic tonight. I am so excited... I want to post everything online, but the less I give away now the better. It keeps the pressure on to keep working.

I got the big table at Starbucks today! AHAHAHAHA!!

AHAHA!

RUB RUB

Thursday, January 21

Possible job offer! A legit one!
!!!

DOUBLE-STUFFED
OREOS
MAAH

Second date! We talked for an hour after the sushi was gone...!! ♡

And in or out of bed
You keep your head wide open
'Cause you don't only dream
When you're asleep
Oh, it was a good day.

Friday, January 22

Bus ride to Portland reminds me why I like the train — BECAUSE IT'S NOT THE BUS. The manchild sitting next to me played motion games with his stupid iPhone THE ENTIRE BUS RIDE (2 hours 15 minutes).
ARE YOU @%!!%ing KIDDING ME RIGHT NOW?!!
bristle
GOLF SWING?!!

I was so excited for Medicine Friday that I left the house without my coat or cell phone! What a dork! I waited at Vault for over an hour because the plan changed and I didn't know.

But! Eventually! MEDICINE FRIDAY!!
SORRY!
On my way out the door!

I feel like I always go home early, but tonight can we have a super late night?
You want to stay out with me all night?!?
YES!!

Drunken sketch group!!

Saturday, January 23

I didn't bring any work to do over the weekend, so I have all the time in the world to...

Follow Mom around as she shops for knitting supplies.

Pet the cat for an hour in front of the fireplace.

...Plus combo points for 17!
?

Play cribbage with Mom and Dad (and learn whatever ridiculous new rules they made up this month).

We went to the Armory to see Snow Falling on Cedars, and a family friend in his first professional role (at the ripe old age of 16). So cool, Connor!!

And then we got Papa Hayden's!!

DROOL...

Sunday, January 24

Met Emi at Coffeehouse Northwest...

Went to Periscope to meet up with Cat...

...And got pizza with David!
Our group keeps growing!!

C'mon — we should get off here.
?
Emi saved me from a Trimet ticket checker!!! That could have sucked soooo bad...! You can get, like, $250 fines for riding MAX without a ticket!

We were the first country to knock Britain down a notch.
Yeah.
I wonder who will do that to us...

China.

Monday, January 25
Doctor's appointment: tonsillectomy successful, no problems 1 month later!
Bought Children of the Sea at Kinokuniya with a gift certificate. I went for the Japanese version so I have to use my Japanese to read the story.
Kai...
Juu...
HUFF
HUFF
Barely caught my train to Eugene!
The snack cart attendant gave me a soda even though I was 50¢ short! Thank you...!!
!
BUMP
BUMP
BUMP
Sitting in class at 9pm, I realized that I am halfway through my senior year. Is this the first twinge of senior sadness? Of not wanting to go?

Tuesday, January 26

This has seriously been the month that Natalie Nourigat got it all.

Go, baby
Go, baby

Ye~ah
we're right
behind you!

ECCC updated its website with a Monsters & Dames page and table assignments!

YES!! We're all together!

Did my homework 2 and 6 days ahead of time. NICE.

THAPT!

Went to the library and printed over 500 sheets of paper for mini-comics. I'm so sorry, everyone else...

HURRY UP!!!!

tap tap

B-but! I went late at night so as not to inconvenience others....!!

Sean Connery Voice Guy!!!

Hello, it is me. Sean Connery. Heh heh heh.

I've still got the moves to sneak past security, heh heh heh.

I came here to say that the service desk will close in 5 minutes.

Connery out.

LOOOOOOL.

snicker

Everyone appreciates Sean Connery Voice Guy.

Wednesday, January 27
Minicomickin'. There's no way that one pair of handscould fold all of this paper in a day... I have to re-member to pace myself!
I went to Kinko's for my mini-comic covers this year. I want some nice, thick paper and no streaks in the ink.
NOD
Scheduled a haircut for next week. But what to have done? Trim, or much shorter? Dye it back to natural, or blend in more blonde?
HMM...
Made nachos and took them to Nate's, where we watched Star Wars: A New Hope and The Empire Strikes Back. Fantastic!!
That's no moon...
Your hands are so small!
I think it's yours that are big.

Thursday, January 28

Hayaya, 2 essays due next week...!

And you can change the graphic later if you want...
Don't tempt me, Kinko's man! I want one really badly, but I need to save my money!

Bought a light for my bike! Yay, not getting run over at night!

Late night printing. People audibly mocked my art as it came out of the printer. I waited to pick it up until they left the printing area, but they still saw me with it and snickered.
RAGE

Friday, January 29

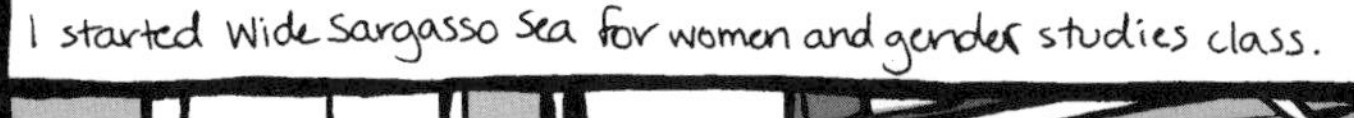
I started Wide Sargasso Sea for women and gender studies class.

Hated Jane Eyre

Got drinks with Alex. We were joined by Gordon, Briana, Meg, John, and Brian.
CHEERS!

I drew a second Witch of Wiheim illustration that is alright.
Is this good enough to be a print...?
Hmm...

Today wasn't very productive, actually. I have a lot to do in the next month!!

I gotta step it up, make a list, and move down it every day.

Saturday, January 30

I cleaned the house ALL. DAY.
Stupid, messy little house!!!
✓sweep and mop floors
✓Beat carpet with broom??
✓Wipe down kitchen
✓Wipe down bathroom
✓Wash bedding, towels
✓Clean mirrors, windows
✓Take out trash
✓Buy candles

Come on in!
sparkle
sparkle
feigned calm
barely finished in time

Sunday, January 31

Carrie is in town, so we met up and walked around town and talked ♡

I used my hour-at-a-time method to work through freelance art, an essay, and a reading assignment. It makes being productive so much easier...

I'm falling into a nice rhythm in Eugene. School, domestic life, art... it's all getting very comfortable and familiar.

I tried using UStream to broadcast an inking session. Very strange... It's hard to get a good view of the art, and I have no idea what to say.

cough

Signed up for a free Netflix trial.

This is a trap, isn't it. It's always a trap...

I bet that they charge you if you don't have the DVDs back in 2 weeks, and they encourage you to make a long queue so they keep coming after the deadline... right?

It's always a trap....!!

Monday, February 1

Canceled the 'free' Netflix trial.
What the fuck is this $10 charge from Netflix?!!

Called customer service about it:
That's just to make sure that your account is valid. You'll see the charge fall off within a week.
It's still a trap. Totally a trap.
Oooh.... Thank you.
Maybe I will try it again someday.... sorry, Netflix.

We watched 'Kairo' in Kurosawa film class tonight, and I am going to go ahead and say that it is one of the scariest movies I have ever seen. I talked through most of it with Sean, because that helped me deal with the terror, but we were so loud that the girl in front of us turned around and actually said:
. . .
SHUSH, omigod.

Aw, HELL yes!!!
Interview for JET, next Friday at 10:00AM!!!! Perfect!!! Some people have interviews in the middle of the week, and have to go to Portland and come back in 1 day, but I can stay for the weekend if I like, and I won't even miss class for it!

Tuesday, February 2

Well, I was going to ask you for another short cut, but... I have this job interview next week and I think I should just get a trim in case they're looking for a conservative appearance.

Reveal!
Yup. (snoozer...)

(Answering yet another question incorrectly)
Sometimes I worry that I ate bad meat like 10 years ago and Mad Cow is finally starting to show. My brain is just not up to speed some days!

Walked home from Japanese lit. with Morgan. That lady cracks me up!
I have a 6-foot Michelangelo in my car.
Like from Ninja Turtles.
Wanna see it?
UMM... YES.

Gym with Hannah and Dana! They tried to call and tell me to come out, but, as usual, my phone was dead.
NAT-A-LIEEE!!
!!

Late-night grocery shopping with Hannah! We planned a 3-in-1 party.
Cheese, wine, mush-room, beef, and make-up party! It has to happen!!
EEEEEEEE

Wednesday, February 3

Thesis Day! I drew over the Surface pages 6 and 7 and inked them live on UStream.
progress....
progress....

I can't hang out this week. :(
Next week?
Yes, please!

It's funny, but I am very picky about the clothes that I draw in.

- Hair out of my face
- No long necklaces and NO rings or bracelets
- 3/4-length-sleeved shirts
- Tight fit through torso so shirts don't rub against wet ink
- Comfy and loose pants

My favorite drawing outfit looks insane...a plaid shirt and pink, knee-length sweat pants! Plus a headband, of course. I AM STYLE.

Road trip to Wondercon with Emi in April? Sounds AMAZING!!!
skip
skip

I was suddenly overwhelmed by how much I have to do. The thesis, preparing for conventions, job searching, freelance art projects, essays, midterms, reading, cooking and cleaning, working out, a man friend...I really felt like assuming the fetal position for a while.

Thursday, February 4

I didn't get much sleep last night.
BEEP
BEEP
BEEP
Can I just skip life today?
BEEP
I kept talking in my head and running through interview scenarios for J.E.T.

Another essay due today! The stress has been constant this week. Hopefully I will get a break after I turn this in.
STA——RE
SHAKE

Japanese lit. professor made us feel really guilty about not doing the reading.

SIIIIIIIIIIIIIIIIIIIIIIIIIIINK....

Had 3 long phone conversations with friends today. I love my friends so much!!

Aw.

Molly

...

Aw.

Jamie

Aw.

Paul

My friends!

Friday, February 5
Thursday T.V. show catch-up on Hulu!!
A HA HA HA HA!!
CLAP CLAP CLAP CLAP CLAP CLAP CLAP CLAP CLAP CLAP CLAP
Secret Half Hour Fist Technique! I do half hour chunks of difficult tasks, rendering them accomplishable.
3 more long phone conversations with friends today.
Okay, REALLY... This is nice, but no more!....
Beep
Watched Scamper the Penguin, a favorite childhood movie of mine. ♡♡

Saturday, February 6

Lots of reading catch-up to do before the Japanese lit. midterm on Tuesday. I got a headache from reading so much on my laptop.

Hannah took me to WOW Hall to see her cousin perform. We stayed for the next act, Betty and the Boy, and it was such a good decision!
Oh my ghost...
WOW.
come with me...
NOD

We followed that up with drinks at Rennie's.
You should try to sabotage my JET application so I have to stay here and live with you.

...And then we went to Safeway to buy bacon and wine...
Is it bacon time?
YES!!
y'know, in case anyone wasn't sure how drunk we were...

...And then we made bacon, got schwastey-faced on wine, and watched Cloudy with a Chance of Meatballs.
BA HA
HA HA
HA
HA
STE——VE!!

Sunday, February 7

I thought about the band we saw last night, and how I think that they will make it big if they can just last - I mean, keep performing without recognition until that finally comes. They have to keep doing little shows and hoping that people will spread their music on blogs and mixCDs, little by little.

Even though it's a different industry, I think it's the same with comics. If you're good, it's just a matter of time before you make it; you just have to have the endurance to last when you have no recognition for years and years, meaning that it has to be rewarding for you even without that.

Productive art and homework day!
IZ GOOD GIRL
Also, I am proud that I didn't spend a cent today!

Called home and talked to Mom and Dad. Why weren't the boys there to talk...?
?

Awakened byyyyy... A droning voice... I love your long shadows and your gunpowder eyes...
typa
type
RUSTLE
Oops! I think I woke up Niha...! Bad roommate...!!

Monday, February 8
Coffee with Darcie! We walked to the river and talked about boys, careers, and living in Portland.
Vintage shopping! New dress and jacket for less than $40.
In Kurosawa film class, the movie was not only not scary — I really, really liked it! Bright Future is a must-see!! Also: A on my film paper! や,た!

Tuesday, February 9

Japanese Lit. midterm! So scary! I studied for over 4 hours today.

...And good thing. That test was HARD. In one section, we were given a single sentence and had to identify the story it came from, author, character speaking, and the sentence's significance in the story.
tap

I got an A- on the paper for that class, so I feel a little safer.
A little .....

Went out for drinks at Taylor's with Nate, Hannah and her friend Oleg, and Dana and her friend Matt.

I'll get the next round.

$1 Wells

Druuunk.

I'll get the next round!!

I'LL GET THE NEEXSHT ROUND!!

SHE BRINGS HOME HER PAY—

FOR LOVE!!

Wednesday, February 10

Ordered prints! So scary... They are expensive and I have had bad luck selling them before, but hopefully these new illustrations at a bigger size will be popular.

S- Surely...

I'm pretty shy, and I like to think that I'm polite, but I can be a bitch when the time is right.

One thing that really bothers me is when people walk towards me in a group and don't leave room for me on the sidewalk. I don't ask for much — just don't walk shoulder-to-shoulder in a group of 3 and expect me to stand in the mud and wait for you to pass.

?

SQUISH

I like to pretend that I don't see that we are going to collide; people almost never realize until the last second that they have to move, and the results amuse me.

Okay............
I think I'm ready.
papers checked (x10)
bag packed
interview outfit inspected
I take a bus home tomorrow, and my JET interview is the next day...!

Thursday, February 11

Mom: Just emailing to make sure you really don't want to go to Sun Valley with us for Spring Break.
Nope...
I feel guilty for skipping a family vacation, but I should work on my thesis that week...

Make-up homework assignments =
BVUH!
I DON'T WANNA!

Long, long trek to the train in the cold.
An old school friend spotted me walking past his work building and popped out to say 'hi'.
I saw you walking by in your coat with your suitcase. You look like a Miyazaki character!
Comparing me to Miyazaki/ Miyazaki characters: ALWAYS APPRECIATED

はじめまして...
More restless sleep before the interview...

Friday, February 12

J.E.T. interview! Woke up at the crack of dawn, checked my papers 5 times, and made myself up to the best of my abilities. Got there 10 min early, met the other interviewees, and had the first interview, which was nice.

I have no idea how I did or if I'll get the job, but it was a good experience! It also feels amazing to have it out of my hands now — I did all I could and the ball is in someone else's court.

Met Mom at Nordstrom Rack for some shopping, but left empty-handed. I was looking for 2 trends I want to hop (Oxford booties and high-heeled sandals), but no luck. ⍨ To the internets!!!

Now it's Emi, Tally and me in sketch group.

Do you guys have a name yet?

Studio Fetus.

...Joking!

Oh, good.

I was like, "Uuuhhh..."

Met Angie at Coffeetime for sketch group, then took her to see Periscope.

Ron's birthday! FLAMING VOLCANO BOWL !!!!!!!!!!!!!!
Hung out with Emi, Jamestown, + Doox.
Hey, ladies.
EIGHTEEN!!

Saturday, February 13
Locked myself out of the house on accident! I had to climb a ladder up to the roof, find an unlocked 2nd story window, and remove the screen.
FAIL.
Ran around Beaverton buying things:
Animator's Survival Kit from Powell's
Highlight Kit from Ulta
Valentine's Day gifts from See's Candies
I saw mini me at the mall!
FWIP
Long, long journey home.

Sunday, February 14

I'm behind on EVERYTHING. Homework, e-mails, text messages, art.... !!

Burned my DiGiorno pizza in the house's ghetto 70's oven in less than even the minimum bake time. Hungry and angry, ARGH!!

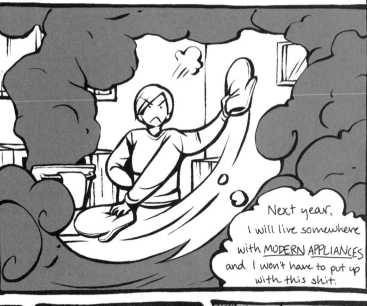

Next year, I will live somewhere with MODERN APPLIANCES and I won't have to put up with this shit.

Why do I feel this way?

Monday, February 15
Stumptown exhibitors' list is up, but I'm not on it! Panic!!
Less than 4 weeks to Emerald City Comicon! I still have 9 pages and a cover to make for Over the Surface 1, 14 pages to color for Larsha, 2 linoleum prints, and an empty portfolio.
GAH!
RIFLE
Nate got me daifuku for Valentine's Day. They are delicious! Every time I eat one I think of him. 花よりだんご indeed!
The way to my heart is through my stomach!
Left in the middle of this week's Kurosawa film (Doppelgänger). My time would be better spent working on Larsha or my homework!

Tuesday, February 16

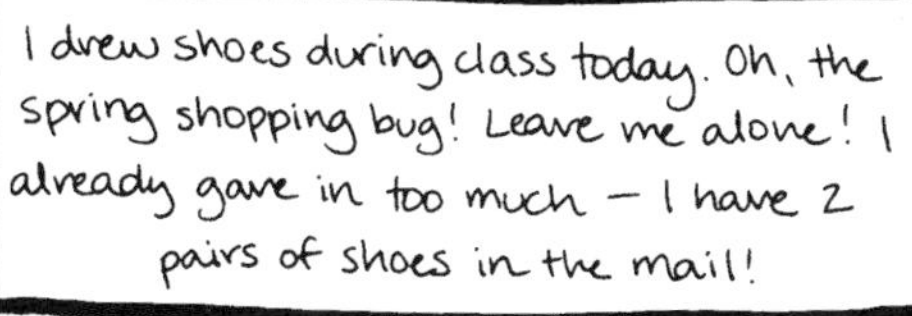
I drew shoes during class today. Oh, the spring shopping bug! Leave me alone! I already gave in too much – I have 2 pairs of shoes in the mail!

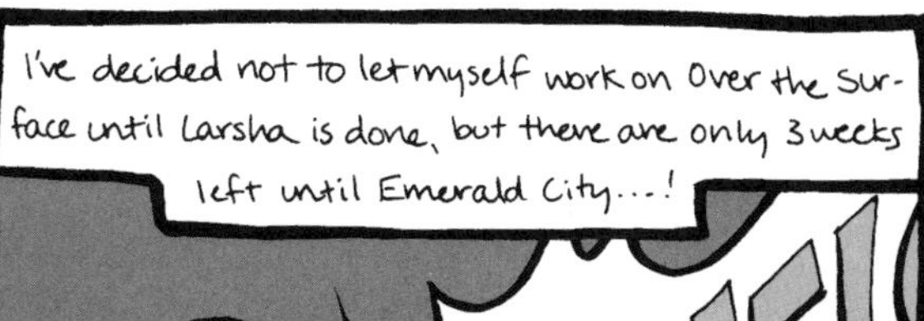
I've decided not to let myself work on Over the Surface until Larsha is done, but there are only 3 weeks left until Emerald City...!

TONE!

Drinks with Nate's friends!
I invited guys, too....
It's OK!

Unfortunately...
Apparently it's Mardi Gras...!
Heh!
...drinks were 4X as expensive as we expected!

Wednesday, February 17
Still coloring...
Coloring...
Coloring...
Thesis registration is up online.
Good God.
Am I on track for this?!
Ran into Jacquie on the street.
Where have you been???
I swear I'll be back all the time spring term!
I really plan to be; with just 8 credits and no con prep next term, I should be able to make it to Pi Phi regularly.
High School Musical dance break:
I WANT IT ALL!!

Thursday, February 18
wo-o-oah,
For the longest time
Once I thought my innocence was gone/ Now I know that happiness goes on/ That's where you found me when you put your arms around me/ I haven't been there for the longest time
...The greatesst miracle of all
Is how I need you, and how you needed me, too
that hasn't happened for the longest time
Maybe this won't last very long
But you feel so right
And I could be wrong
Maybe I've been hoping too hard
But I've come this far
And it's more than I'd hoped for
Who knows how much further we'll go on
Maybe I'll be sorry when you're gone
I'll take my chances
I forgot how nice romance is
I haven't been there for the longest time
I had second thoughts at the start
I said to myself, 'Hold on to your heart'
Now I know the woman that you are
You're wonderful so far
And it's more than I'd hoped for
I don't care what consequence it brings
I have been a fool for lesser things
I want you so bad, I think you ought to know that
I intend to hold you for the longest time

Friday, February 19

Still... coloring...
...coloring...
...coloring....
Laid out my portfolio and made files for sample prints. My portfolio is HUUUGE... 11" x 17"! Much, much too big....
FWUMP
Finished coloring Larsha!!!!!!!
YES GOD, YES
Am I.... Am I actually ahead of schedule for ECCC....?
FWIP
MURPHY'S LAW

Saturday, February 20
Roomie kitchen clean-up
SPRAY
RUB
NEW SHOES
I got to go to that mountain today.
That's Spencer Butte??!
Yup! That's what we're hiking!
That's... so....
Perfect.
Lately, the theme of my life has been that been that I'm in a place I didn't imagine I could reach.

Sunday, February 21
Woke up when Nate left, and then slept until noon!
Bye!♥
Bye♥
Drew the Over the Surface 1 cover, but it is 2" too big for my scanner!
A black cat crosses my path pretty regularly...
...which is what happens, I guess, when you live next door to one.
How was your day?
Good, but not as good as yesterday.

Monday, February 22

Colored the Over the Surface cover.
Really?? Done in less than a day? Am I getting faster, or lazier...?

Registered for classes! I signed up for 3 Japanese electives (12 credits, the minimum to be on my parents' insurance plan), but I am hoping I can drop 1 when I register to get 4 credits for working on my thesis. I am also in pilates with Hannah and Dana! Yay abs and gossip!

You will go and you will LIKE IT.
FLUBBA
FLUBBA

Printed more A Room of One's Own minis in the library. I hate backing up the printers, but it's so cheap...! How could I go anywhere else...?

scratch

hah....
hah....

Watched Loft in Kurosawa class. Everyone else was laughing, but I was really scared! Ghosts and mummies and swamps... yuckers!

Tuesday, February 23

Reading Under the Feet of Jesus for Women and Gender Studies. It's sooooo good!! I can't believe how contemporary it is, though... Terrifying that people are living like that at this very moment.

What is wrong with me today?? I had a good sleep, good breakfast, and my normal cup of coffee, but I'm exhausted. It's a fight to stay awake 2-6pm.

BZZZZZZZT

CURE: Dance party to Whitney Houston's Step by Step. The lyrics speak to me during this convention preparation crunch.

You've gotta keep on moving—

DON'T STOP!

LOST is on, but I am watching The Bachelor: The Women Tell All.
OH MY GOOOODDD... SHUT UPPP
Why the HELL do I not have cable?!

Wednesday, February 24

Thesis Day...has kind of gotten off track. I have re-prioritized several times in the last 8 weeks, putting hw and freelance before the thesis. But! Now it's back to Fer Reals Thesis Day!!!!!

FER REALS

Picked up Joëlle Jones and David Hahn's Madame Xanadu issues!
DING
♡

Printed the 75 Over the Surface linoleum prints! Sooo fun...takes me back to high school art classes.

peel

Kinko's Man is incredulous. He is surprised that I have an order to pick up and raises his eyebrows when he tells me the total price.
I MAKE IT RAIN, FOOL!
UHN!
CLATTER
SLIDE MY DAMN CARD!!

Went out for $1 beers with Hannah and Dana, but there was a cover and the bouncer had no change.
The cover is only until 11:00...
shrug
Okay, well... we'll be back.
It looked like our I.D.'s had been rejected or something, though. I was embarrassed.

Thursday, February 25

DEADLINES
It is an epic race against time.
Today's PUMP UP SONG:
Hot - Missy Elliott
Perhaps less relevant than step by step, but oooooh so fun.
Hatas I flip the bird.
Got guns? So what— I ain't scared.
TUG
Inked over the Surface page 8 and toned it.
I think I can...
I think I can
I think
I t
Decided on May 12 for my thesis defense. Dear God, is that enough time...?

Friday, February 26

I stayed inside, in my PJs, ALLLLLLLLLL DAAAAAAAAAAAAY.

*

I printed 75 copies of the Between Gears linoleum print in a single go, and had to get creative about where to dry them in our tiny house...

HAAAAND.

Today's PUMP UP SONG: Bad Romance - Lady Gaga

Saturday, February 27
Beautiful day! Even the bees are out.
I lined paper for Over the Surface and went into a reverie about my time volunteering at a nursing home. I cried and cried as I went over a painful experience from that time.
大切なものにいつか もしも気づいた時に...
Today's PUMP UP SONG: 孤独のシグナル from Serial Experiments Lain
I took the night off to hang out with Nate. We made dinner at his apartment and watched Firefly with his friends. Wonderful night!
I could talk all day about how great Nate is, but I don't want to embarrass him. Just trust me when I say he's a stand-up guy.
Which Deadly Sin do you think you are?
....
Wrath?
Wrath?!
I have no idea.
H-how about you?

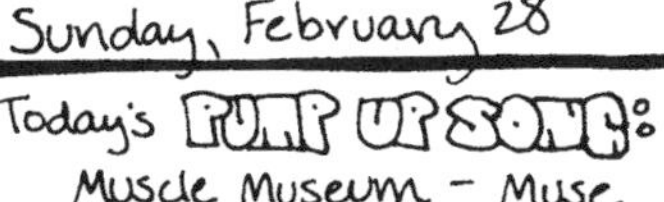
Sunday, February 28

Today's PUMP UP SONG: Muscle Museum - Muse

DANANANA
NANANA
AIR-STRUM

Drew page 10 of Over the Surface from start to finish and penciled 11! New record for pages drawn in a day!

I thought that growing up meant becoming a different person, but it hasn't for me. I still feel like myself, though I recognize the changes that have come with age.

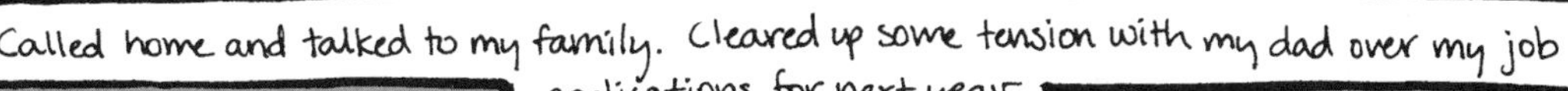
Called home and talked to my family. Cleared up some tension with my dad over my job applications for next year.

I just want you to know: I know that you are just trying to help me, and I know that it will be good for me to apply for a lot of jobs, but I didn't have time this week, I won't have time next week, and I think that spring break would be a good time to do more.

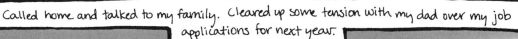

I am the only one of my friends who has applied for more than one job, and only a few have applied for one yet at all! Jeez! I know it's tough love, but I am over my head already with my other responsibilities.

Monday, March 1
Today's PUMP UP SONG: Bop to the Top – H.S.M.
Baby to be #1
You've got to
raise the bar!
Finished page 11 of Over the Surface, got halfway through 12.
Ideal breakfast:
COFFEE
Ideal Lunch:
2 ( ) + O.J.
I could eat the same thing for breakfast and lunch every day and be happy.
American Apparel t-shirt and hoodie
Joe's jeans
Uggs
North Face fleece
brand whore
Lately, it is so much warmer outside at night.
It smells wonderful, like wet flowers.

Tuesday, March 2

Today's PUMP UP SONG: I'm Your Daddy - Weezer

You've got the brains, the body and the beauty

To top it off you've cool

Barely made it to JPN 399, and then I almost fell asleep...!

.....

I have not been very responsible this week.

The reading for this week is 87 pages...

...

AAAAA AAAA!

Wednesday, March 3
Where would you go? Not long ago I've been thinking out loud
Finished page 13 of Over the Surface by 3:00.
Today's PUMP UP SONG: Lasso – Phoenix
I treated myself to a shower, makeup, and the latest LOST episode.
Oh, yes. My face with makeup. I forgot how that looked...
Tried on outfits for an hour. I do so love clothes.
Strikin' weird poses, WHOO! →
I kept drawing late into the night... I may actually be able to finish Over the Surface 1 tomorrow!!
Trying to follow your ideal Oh sorry but your so-called life it is such a waste
RESPONSIBLE SIDE APPROVES

Thursday, March 4

Finished the last 3 Over the Surface pages today.
PUMP UP SONG:
Ashes - Embrace
Now watch me rise up and leave all the ashes you made out of me!
-zip!

Went to the library to print minicomic pages at 3AM. I HATE walking alone at night, man. It's not fair. I want an invisibility cloak so I can go around in the dark without a worry. It would be fun if I didn't have to worry about other people harassing me.
Hey, why you walking so fast?
Why do I have to keep my head down and take this shit?

I wonder what it would feel like to be the only person awake in the city at 4 in the morning.
Kind of cool, scary, and lonely all at once, I imagine.

Came home at 4 and passed out.

Friday, March 5

CLANG-
A-
LANG-

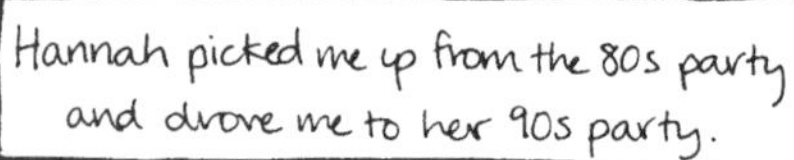
Biked to the liquor store and back. It felt very 'college'.

I still get nervous when I walk into a liquor store. It's the same as walking through sensors in stores; I KNOW I'm not shoplifting, but the fact that someone is questioning me makes me feel guilty.

Can I help you?
I'M 22!
I-I mean... I'm fine. Thank you...

Went to Nate's friends' house to help set up for their 80's party.

Hannah picked me up from the 80s party and drove me to her 90s party.

I biked to the liquor store today, and it was like, 'CLANGALANG', and I was all, 'Yeah, that's vodka. You wish you were 21.'

Okay. I believe Natalie is drunk.

We were deplorable drunks tonight. We went to Safeway at 1:30 for donuts and cheese nips.
GASP!* CAKE!!
Natalie, get up. GET UP.
PFFFAHAHAHA!!
LOLS

This Safeway is open until 2 for a reason, though. I'm not surprised that we were allowed to stay.

Saturday, March 6

The walk of shame is shameful, even when you didn't sleep with anyone.
Bright...
So bright....

The sun was out and it was actually warm! It isn't possible to overstate the beauty of sunshine and falling cherry blossoms. I could stay outside all day just staring up at the cherry trees.

Now that Over the Surface 1 is done, I just have to finish one extra page for Larsha, 2 final projects for school, and then I can get back to Between Gears pages.

Haha, oh man! How long has it been...?

Six weeks. SIX. WEEKS.

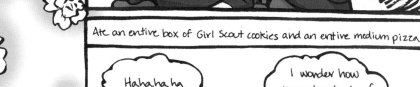

Ate an entire box of Girl Scout cookies and an entire medium pizza.

Hahahaha, oh man!
I wonder how many hundreds of calories that was!
SOB

Sunday, March 7

Still feel sick from the pizza and Girl Scout cookies.
BWOOF.

Very unproductive day, unfortunately. I may be in the clear for con prep, but I still have responsibilities!

Picked up prints at Kinko's and finished organizing my portfolio.

Mom and Neil couldn't come to Eugene today as planned, but Mom says she'll come down on Thursday to go for a hike, grab lunch, and drive me to Portland.
Well, hey! That sounds pretty great.

Monday, March 8

Push up, overload, legendary heavy glow

Listening to Gorillaz's Stylo on repeeeeat. That flow is bomb.

Last night of Kurosawa class! The film was Tokyo Sonata, which made me cryyyyy.... I get heart-poundingly protective of little boy characters (big sister syndrome), so this one was really hard for me to watch.

CHOKE
Drip
Drip
Drip
QUIVER
THUMP
THUMP
CLENCH

Yes, what happened to Ryuuhei?
He got railed by a fucking van.

What's that?
...
SNORT

I will miss one thing about Kurosawa class, and that is Sean and my running commentary.

I'm out.
WHYYY??!
I hate that guy.

I'm drawing portraits of my favorite Parks and Recreation characters saying my favorite quotes. It is so ridiculously fun ♡

Tuesday, March 9

I had a nightmare that I was at ECCC without half of my merchandise!
NOOOOO!!

Pro Registration opened for San Diego Comic-Con!!!
Can I afford to go this year...?
Hmm
Picked up a little table banner that I ordered from Kinko's.
Dinky, but cute.

I never pursued the Rihanna/Chris Brown abuse story, but I finally watched the Diane Sawyer interview. I admire Rihanna a lot, and this interview is a great example of why. It seems like people want to see a certain 'victim' image, but she is level-headed and classy despite prodding.
It was a wake-up call.
It was a wake-up call for me...
...big time.

Wednesday, March 10

Date with Nate! Dinner at cornucopia. I got a very messy halibut burger.

I'd say, "Try some!" but I kind of destroyed it...

drip

I'm good.

...Then Alice in Wonderland. My first 3D movie!!

GRIN

Let me see this...

NICE.

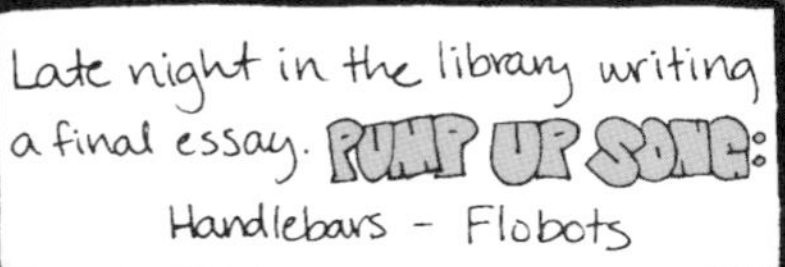
Late night in the library writing a final essay. PUMP UP SONG:
Handlebars - Flobots

I can design an engine
64 miles to the gallon of gasoline

Thursday, March 11
Finished my essay early in the morning. I am finally feeling the burden of school lifting.
RUB
RUB
Mom came to Eugene to get lunch together and drive me to Portland.
I won a $5 token! Can you use this?
GASP!
The ONE...!
We had the luxury of stopping in Woodburn to shop - I even found the sheath dress I've been searching for all year! BCBG outlet for the win!
I spent time with the family tonight instead of going to a Top Shelf party with Emi. It was a tough choice, but I needed to catch up with everyone! I often breeze in and out of town without spending time with the fam, but not this weekend!
HS

Friday, March 12

Running LATE!!!!!! How could I prepare so much this year and still be scrambling to finish in time??
Also, why do I have so much stuff?! When Mom picked up my suitcase, she just looked at me and asked,
Really?
FWIP
'Bye, Portland!
'Bye, Oregon!
Road trippin' with my ladies! ♡
We got into Seattle at 3:30 and had time to be tourists.

I got some time with Joëlle to relax and catch up in the hotel room. She poured me some of her nice vodka and we sat in the lovely sunset and chatted. Just what I needed!

Took a load of stuff over to the convention center with Jamie.

Come on, Tally.

Give me one hot minute!

clomp clomp

Emi and I were in bed by 10:30, asking cheesy sleepover questions like "What TV star would you marry?"

You guys are LAME.

Whatever.

DIDN'T.
SLEEP.
A WINK.

Saturday, March 13

Had a HORRIBLE walk to the convention center today with 2 trips' worth of things. Matt saved me by taking my minicomic box, but the rest of my stuff was still way too heavy and awkward. I was dying!

HUFF

I got to the con sweaty and exhausted, with very little time to set up. We split a table 3 ways, which was NOT enough room, and I had to erase the title of the print at the beginning of all 75 Over the Surface minis because apparently it was a euphamism for a certain part of male anatomy. Not the best start to my day!

Lots of people came by to have their Monsters & Dames books signed, and I got some of the sweetest comments from people saying that mine was their favorite. One guy told me that he read the book with his wife and 5-year-old daughter, and they all stopped to talk about mine. Some people said that they were moved to tears, which I nearly was hearing about it.

Angie introduced Emi and me to Brandon Graham, who was so friendly and awesome! I have followed his work since he was publishing through Tokyopop in 2007, and I had to try really hard to not be a shameless fangirl.

! ! !
WOOOOAH....
King City originals

CHEERS!

We went to dinner at Baguette Box and had drinks at White Horse Trading co. The food, company, and conversation were all excellent. Great night!

Drunk dialed Nathan!
Ah miss youuu! K bai!

We had an epic sleepover party in our hotel room, where at one point all 4 girls were in 1 bed and quotes included:

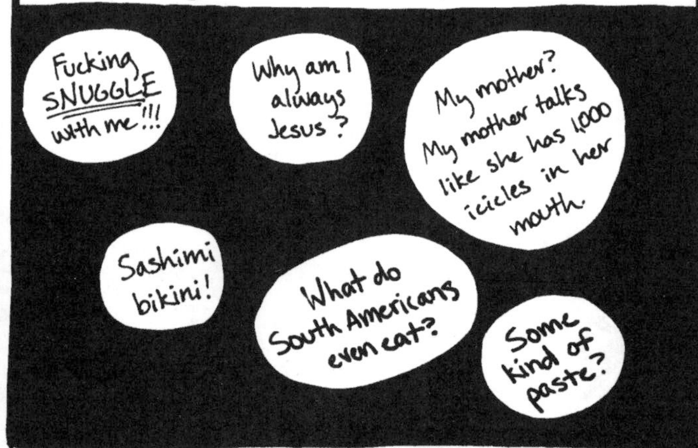

Fucking SNUGGLE with me!!!
Why am I always Jesus?
My mother? My mother talks like she has 1,000 icicles in her mouth.
Sashimi bikini!
What do South Americans even eat?
Some kind of paste?

Sunday, March 14
Emi and I were able to get around the floor a bit more today. One of my favorite people I talked to was Angela Melick of Wasted Talent, who traded her adorable buttons for a Between Gears mini, and explained how she gets such nice colors in her comics and preserves them while scanning.
By 6:00, my brain was DEAD. I just stood around staring off into space for minutes at a time.
...
Tally, you have this, "What do I do now?" expression on your face...
We wanted to shop at H+M after dinner, but they close early on Sunday!
Hmm... I think it's closed...
I don't want to look knowing that I can't go in...!
But I see people in there!
...
But apparently Portland is getting one this summer, so I feel like I can survive.
Starbucks kept Emi and me awake on the drive home. We explained to each other in-depth the long-form comics that we want to make someday.
It's going to happen. We just have to stick with it.
I believe in the three of us.
Zzzz...
Cons are so inspiring!! When I see the cool things that other artists are doing, I just want to get back to work and produce something as great as what they're doing.
What should I even draw first?!!

Monday, March 15

Super, DUPER sore body from all of the box moving and tense table posture this weekend.

LOLL
LOLL
LOL
PURR

What Not to Wear with Mom. ♡

BAM

So many comics to read!!!!!!!!!!

I finally pimped out my art bag w/ buttons like I've been meaning to. Favorite is my Brittney Lee Emi/Angie/Tally friendship button.

!!!

Ran errands in the Subaru. Was delighted when I turned on the radio just as Short Skirt Long Jacket started.

Watched Bright Future a second time before starting my JPN 410 paper on it. I sounded so dumb trying to explain it to Mom...

And then the rest of the movie is those middle schoolers walking toward the camera in a wandering herd!
Hm!

I feel smothered by all of the good things in my life right now.

The hardest decisions are the ones that make you choose between two good things, and that is my life right now.

Tuesday, March 16
It looks like I am really going to have a graphic novel job next year (knock on wood)! What will this mean for JET? Nate? My living situation? I am so ready to be back on the ground and sure of my plans....
Fast spider on the couch, AHHH! I button-mash-kicked until I finally got it.
SMUSH SMUSH SMUSH
Jeff and Jamie both told me to come out tonight and meet a talent scout from Marvel. They really have my back, time and again. I am so lucky and grateful for the people who have decided to help me in comics!
brag brag brag brag brag
fidget!
pat pat
brag brag brag brag brag
fidget!
pat pat
WORDS OF WISDOM FROM RICH
You're thinking about things the right way. Even the things you're worried about — you're worrying about them the right way.
We stayed late and talked about movies, restaurants...
La la la la la la la
...and strip clubs.

Wednesday, March 17

Got back from the bar last night really late, woke up early today, and started studying for my JPN 399 final. I left for Eugene at 11 and sang myself silly on the drive down.
I REALLY LOVED BREAKING YOUR HEART!!

I feel so unprepared for this test, but I made my choices and now it's time to face the music. I got a 97% on the midterm and 100% on the final paper, so I hope that will save me from being screwed if it goes terribly.
I just want a C...! Senioritis has made me the laziest student ever.

I set up a fan page for myself on Facebook, and I am so moved by some of the people I haven't talked to in years becoming fans.
Aw!

Met up with Nate, walked by the river.

Laid down on the grass and talked about our childhoods.

Looked for 4-leaf clovers in the park.
We didn't find any.
We'll make our own luck.

We went to Rennie's for drinks, then back to Nate's for a fun, small party.
My goal is to wake up feeling like P-Diddy.
Dana

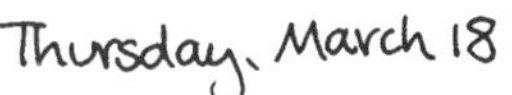
Thursday, March 18

I loved waking up with you.

Drove back to Portland in a daze. Couldn't stop thinking about sex, why I haven't had or wanted it, and wondering what's wrong with me. I tried singing to take my mind off of it, but...

I wanna f*** you like an ♫ animal—
Nooooooo.
SHUDDER
CLICK!

I stayed in a weird mindset all day. My brain feels utterly fried from ECCC, insufficient sleep this week, the night at The Moon and Sixpence, my JPN 410 final paper, and the JPN 399 final.

Met Jamie and Emi at Silk for dinner and drinks. Jamie filled me in on something REALLY important that I didn't pick up on Tuesday!!!
What?!
WHAT?!!
Nod!

We went to Powell's for a nightcap and looked through the comics.
Oh YEAH?? Where's your comic?
It's going to be right HERE!
Mine is going to be at eye-level.
(You Have Killed Me)

Friday, March 19

Nick told me that on New Years 3 years ago, the only time I ever smoked pot, he swapped it out for pipe tobacco.
I wasn't going to let you smoke pot.
REALLY??

Maybe he's just messing with me, but I choose to believe it.
Wow. So I've never done drugs.
...I feel absolved.
PS - how funny is it that my little brother protects me from the dangers of drugs?? ♡

Went downtown for a Periscope fix.
Somewhere, a child is dying because of you.
NOOOOOO!!
I got teased for selling my Monsters and Dames original for profit. I didn't know about the auction!!

MEDICINE FRIDAY!!

Shanghai, then Sushi Land. It is a winning combo, we have found.

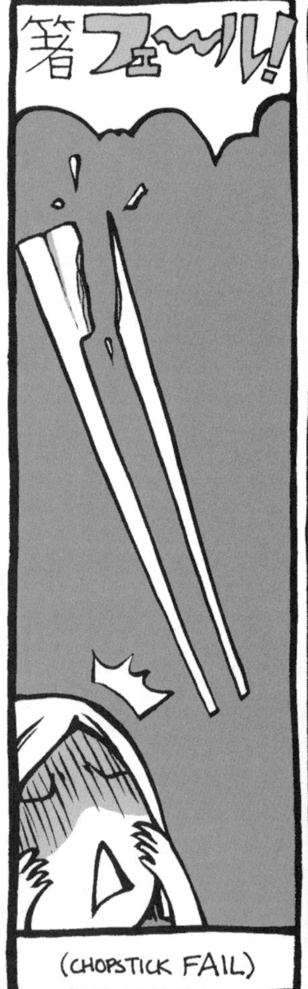

箸フェール!
(CHOPSTICK FAIL)

Everything has started happening for us THIS WEEK!!
I knew we could do it if we kept at it!
We're going to be the people that we look up to now.
And we have to treat new artists the way that they've treated us.

Saturday, March 20

Reread a pitch from last summer. The first time I opened it, I immediately closed it again because it was so embarrassing.
Oh Lord.
wince

Had to help Mom, Nick, and Neil move Grandma Cay out of her nursing home (she was evicted! :\) We took 4 car trips in 3 hours. It was difficult, but problem solving as a family was really good for us.
Oh! We can just slide it out of its groove!

Went to Periscope with Emi and met Cat and Ron there. I felt really bad, because the 4 of us coming in was my idea, but I was really late because of moving.
Sorry, guys...

Went to coffee with Erika and Matt. They're great.♡ I talked with them about comic projects, living in Portland, and got advice on some things I had questions about. I also learned what a 'Juggalo' is!

Went to It's Complicated with Mom at The Valley. Very funny movie!

It's great to see a woman that age, looking her age, totally beautiful and with her own thing going on. Did you see her kitchen and garden?!

I slapped at a fly in my room and it hit the floor dead.

Sunday, March 21

Went to sketch group at Coffee Time. We couldn't get a booth, but the company made up for the lack of space. Emi inadvertently created a new Between Gears spin-off:

Between Screws!!

It could be an autobio about someone's love life!

PFFF

It feels like things have come together for sketch group very suddenly. Each of us has something big in the pipeline!

I'm so proud of us!!!

Are you ready to be home alone?
I've got my socks all ready!

For my Risky Business dance.
GROSS.

Monday, March 22
♪ Just take those old records off the shelf! ♪
slide,
House-sitting this week!!!!!!!!!!!!
Paul came over and we watched Infomania and The Soup just for clips from Dinashark.
Is that a shark?!
Nope! It's a DINO-SHARK!!
WE HAVE TO SEE THIS.
We walked to Starbucks and drew for a while. It was so nice out that I got an ICED soy latte!
NUMMERS.
Sketch group again with Terry and Emi!
-RING- Ooh! It's Nate!!
LOL.
GONE!

Tuesday, March 23

Went to Periscope again. ü Walking back to my car, I passed the Tiffany Center and thought back on prom. Has it already been four years? I feel so different now...

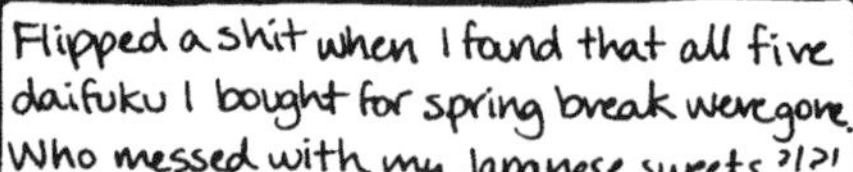
Where will I be in four more years?

Hot Tub Time Machine screening with Jamie.
That was.... entertaining.
Arguably.

Crazy college times with Hannah and Dana in my empty house.
MAH!
(skittles)
HA
HA HA!

Flipped a shit when I found that all five daifuku I bought for spring break were gone. Who messed with my Japanese sweets?!?! Because I WILL END YOU.

Wednesday, March 24

Ooooog...no partying to-night, please... my body needs a day off.
BROKE'D

Why do I always leave the house looking like a crazy cat person on dentist appointment days...?
Late
late
late!!
(cat hair)

Cleeeeeeean teeth!
And no cavities, YAY.

The cats usually sleep with my brothers, and whenever they are gone, the cats get more and more desperate for affection. It's already pretty bad....
MRAAAAAA
MOW
MOW
MOW
MOOOOW
MOW
M-
MOW
Yes, HI. I'm right here.
Will I survive until Friday...?!!

What should I do now?
OOH! I'll watch Ponyo again! Best! Week! EVER!

Who would you have to see to cry like that girl over Justin Beiber?
Uhm... Tina Fey...?

But really, seeing Miyazaki from 20 feet away last summer pretty much proves that I will never have that reaction, even to my idols.

Thursday, March 25

SNAP!
Oh God...
I have a lotta, lotta, LOTTA work to do today.

SCOTT PILGRIM TRAILER

WOAH.
SUPER windy!

Made a pros and cons list of going to Japan for JET and staying in PDX. Man, now I'm swinging back the other way.... it would be a travel experience not only to enjoy at the time, but to draw from creatively for years to come. I guess it's not worth stressing over until I know whether or not I am on the 'short list' (should be mailed next week).

Went to Terry's to watch Romy and Michelle's high school re-union, Community, and Parks & Rec. He burned me a copy of his Briar Hollow playlist and sent me home with pretty art books!

OM
NOM
NOM

MROW.
The cats are getting really aggressive in their demands for affection. I'm glad this is my last night alone with them!

Friday, March 26

Family comes home tonight, eek! I wasn't crazy with the house, but artifacts from the week might suggest otherwise.
STASH!

Read Starting Point for a while. It is very reassuring somehow. Like, even though Miyazaki calls for the very best in you, it feels like he believes you can do it if you really try.

Brushed up on Pixar as a company in anticipation of Emi and my tour next weekend. Such a bummer that you need a degree in art to apply for their internships...

How am I going to qualify myself for these jobs...?

I guess if I can get a job, any job, in an animation studio, that would be a good start.

When I was little, I loved the movie Homeward Bound. As an homage to the movie, I decided to animate it. I drew the opening shot on printer paper with markers, drew the next shot the same way with the characters moving a little, and then realized just how much effort animation takes. I decided to only draw the important scenes — what was necessary to understand the movie — with single illustrations, and ended up 'inventing' primitive storyboarding. I've always imagined myself really enjoying the work of a storyboard artist.

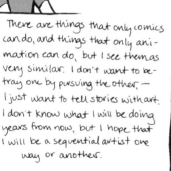

— Oh yeah...

There are things that only comics can do, and things that only animation can do, but I see them as very similar. I don't want to betray one by pursuing the other, — I just want to tell stories with art. I don't know what I will be doing years from now, but I hope that I will be a sequential artist one way or another.

Emi and I went to Blue Moon to talk about comics, studio space, and possibly living together next year.

Hung out with Molly and Paul. ♡ Bought a ticket for Hot Tub Time Machine against my better judgment, but left 20 minutes in.
I'm sorry, guys... I can't do this again.
AWW.

Saturday, March 27

Dad talked to me today about the future. For the first time, he did not mention an ad agency or a salaried job.
For the first time, he thinks I can make it as a full-time artist.
Went downtown to try selling my minis to Portland businesses.
RESULT: 1 out of 3. FTL.
There is something wrong with my brain lately. I'm sluggish, witless, and unmotivated. I hope it's just temporary—senioritis or mental burnout from the busy month—and not some mystery medical issue.

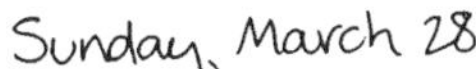
Sunday, March 28

Dad sat me down after breakfast and grilled me about why I haven't applied for more salary jobs. Every time I get my hopes up, I tell you...
I should know by now.

My friends haven't applied for jobs AT ALL —
I have 2 job offers and I've applied for 2 more jobs on top of that!
Fuck this! You've only upset because they aren't good enough for you, but I'm happy with them!
PACE
PACE

Shopping: expensive
Aunt Karin hand-me-downs: free!
New clothes:
• 1 pair shorts
• 1 pair pants
• 3 blouses
• 1 dress
• 3 swimsuits
• 1 purse
• 1 silk scarf
THANKS, AUNT KARIN!! ♡♡♡

Love you.

HORRIBLE TRIP BACK TO EUGENE.

Trains sold out, waited an extra hour for a full bus. Walked home in the rain with 3 bags, laptop bag strap broke and laptop and tablet hit the cement.

gr
grmble
grmble
drip

I use my anger as motivation to work. I feel a little bit more like myself today, and even if it's fueled by a negative emotion, it's good to be back.

SPRING

Monday, March 29

Thumbnailed chapter 2 of Over the Surface.

Man... this is a lot of work....

24 pages, 5 weeks... is this possible...?

Aw, guys... thanks!!

DANG, I've gotten a ton of Etsy sales this week!

Got drinks at Taylor's with a group of Pi Phi's before chapter.

Went to chapter for the first time in MONTHS.
KAAAYLA!!
TALLY!
Workin', workin', workin' away on comics.
How many times have you seen this panel??

Tuesday, March 30

First pilates class! We had a fitness test:
Sit-ups: 1
Push-ups: 6
Wall sit: 2 min
Stretching: fingertips to toes (barely)
FITNESS FAIL
whoo!

First JPN 410 class with Nate and Professor Freedman (my thesis advisor).
We will also talk about reincarnations of stories, fanfiction, and yaoi. I have a lecture with the alternate title, 'Harry Potter did WHAT to WHO?!'
COLLECTIVE GIRL GASP
!!
!!
!!

Met with 2 of my 3 advisors to talk about my thesis.
breathe
It's gonna be okay.....

First JPN 307 class! We watched Swallowtail – sooo good!
Is this.... historically accurate...?
No, dumbass.

Ghetto Oven burned my cookies! Mofo oven bakes only at 450°, no matter what you turn the dial to. 6 min and my cookies are already turning black.
EWW

Date night: Wizard People, Dear Reader!
"You will be schooled here."

Wednesday, March 31
Freaking out about your thesis does not get you any closer to done!
DO THE DAMN THING!
it's too awful...!
too...
awful....
Spent hours trying to get orders ready to send and working on commissions.
Tried on outfits for the San Fran trip tomorrow!
Heather is in town! We lived together last spring, but I haven't seen her in a year. She has been doing Teach for America in NYC.
2 beers and I am DRUUUUNK! Lightweight to the max.
woop
woop
woop!
SSS-
ST-
AGGER
TALLYCHYCK
TEAM
JACOB!
DeviantArt April Fool's Day joke: changing everyone's icons to Twilight, Lady Gaga, etc. gifs. I flipped a shit. I am so gullible sometimes, it's not even funny.
WHAT?!

I am a pretty polite person, but I make exceptions for:
ptoo
GROSS.
Spitting
Have you voted yet?
Yup!
H-oh!...
Did you vote for OSPIRG?
Nope!
Clipboarders
Road trip to San Francisco with Emi!
This is such an adventure!!
Already?
I can sense it!
yeah
yeah
how long must you wait for it...?
オロ?
オロ?
HA HA HA HA HA!
Stayed with Emi's friend Matt and his wife. They have adorable Pomeranians.
LUNA
SOL

Friday, April 2
We drove into SF in the morning. It's so PRETTY!
Emi and I rectified ECCC by hitting up H + M. ◡̈
BE CLEAN!
FRESHEN
HAPPY!
Then we went to Japantown and did purikura.
I got drunk off of one beer and one cider....
Shape up, sorority girl!!!
PIXAR
ANIMATION STUDIOS
Josh Cooley gave Matt, Emi, and me a tour of Pixar. We saw tons of stuff from UP and even got to sit in on a staff film festival.
So, umm....
What do I have to do to work here again....?
Best. Day. EVER!!

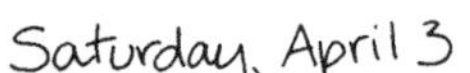
Saturday, April 3

Red one
Blue one
Gray one!
LEAN
We got lunch at Fenton's !!!!!!!!!!!!!

WONDERCON
There's a bird inside.....

Tally, you should ask Josh about Pixar internships!
Oh, I don't know... I feel so awkward talking about it...
You've gotta get over it — this is a great op-portunity.
I know. So why can't I?

Rollerderby match!
Emi and I snuck over the rope and went down the pier to be mis-chievous.

CLOMP
I'm scared....!!!!
CLOMP
We told ghost stories before bed.

Sunday, April 4
Pretty Artist Detective Agency, ASSEMBLE!
There was a snowstorm on the pass! We had a moment of complete blindness when the truck in front of us sprayed our windshield. I may have screamed...
Sploosh
Bumper-to-bumper, snow piling up, no snow tires....
There's a wreck on I-5....
We are NEVER getting home!
Things looked pretty bad, but then-!
You are all safe now.
Molly Muldoon SAVES THE DAY (really)

Monday, April 5

Woke up to an e-mail from Carol Burrell with a contract for the YA graphic novel we have been talking about. (!!)
YES!!
Now to hit up Dad and Erika for contract advice...!

Strange luck lately... some great things have happened, but not without terrible things. I want it to end. Can I take a break from interacting with people and regroup?
spin
spin

I feel better when I get to work. First 12 pages of Over the Surface ch 2 are measured with panel borders drawn. I also wrote out everything I could for the text portion of the thesis.

Dyed my hair light brown. I tried to get it close to its natural color so that I won't have to deal with it for a few months. Coloring is fun, but it's also expensive and time-consuming.

Went to the library with Nate to work on our theses.
sigh
I know.

5 pages written!!!
It's... something!!

Tuesday, April 6

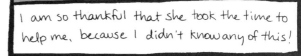

Pilates is difficult!

Kick
Kick
beat
beat

My hair is out of the mushroom stage, into the 90's shag stage.

I am an irregular patron of the campus comic shop. I go in once in a while to find things I'm missing.

Do you have the Mysterius trade?
Sold out.
Sweet Tooth?
Sold out.
. . .
MERR.

Dylan Meconis sent me an e-mail full of amazing legal advice.

THANK YOUUUUU!!

I am so thankful that she took the time to help me, because I didn't know any of this!

Wednesday, April 7

Doing my 50-minute trick to get things done:

Over the Surface

Thesis

Homework

Reading

Holly Golightly.com.

Larsha

Wearing just a zip-up outside at 7PM! It's so beautiful and warm, I can't believe it!!

Thursday, April 8

I made the final JET cut!! Regardless of whether or not I choose to go, it is an honor to be asked.
No one is going to make this decision for me, are they...

I realized that I have been thinking about this choice all along from other people's points of view...staying close for family, to live with friends, going to Japan for Nate or for friends who applied and didn't make it...

What do YOU want?!

. . .

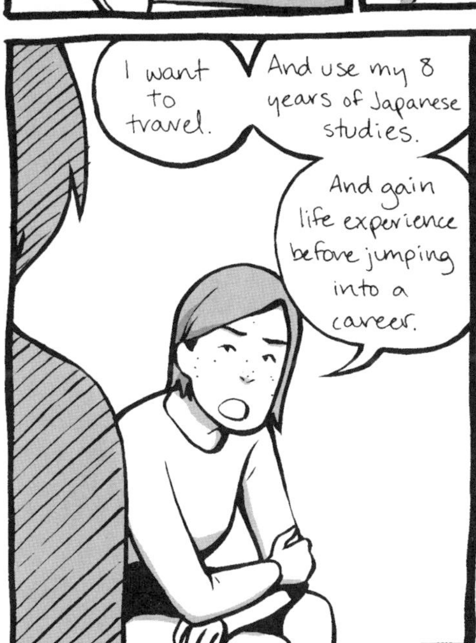
I want to travel.
And use my 8 years of Japanese studies.
And gain life experience before jumping into a career.

But I want to have time to draw comics, too!!
Great! This is the stuff that decisions are made of!

Went to Prince Puckler's and then a fundraiser at Agate Alley with Nate (who is also JET-accepted!). I got to catch up with Darcie and Michelle.
This is your signature thing.
Wha— this??
Glitter Fingers
I guess I do do that a lot....

Friday, April 9

I drew one and a half pages today! I feel like myself again.

...No, really, that's all I did. I drew literally all day and watched things on Hulu for background noise.

Umm... My butt hurts from pilates yesterday?
Today was not eventful ....

I piled clothing onto the foot of my bed and put my Uggs on because it was too cold to fall asleep.

Saturday, April 10

Thesis countdown: 24 days, 21 pages left.
DEADLINE
I don't want a serious relationship. I want to put my energy into art!
HEY. Stop that talk!

This guy is special and you know it. He's given you all the space you need and been more than patient when you don't have time to see him. You're trying to find fault in the relationship because you're afraid of commitment and you don't want to feel accountable to another person.

Also, you are stressed as shit so I forgive you.
Responsible Side has a SOFT SIDE!

Saw Date Night with Kayla. Funny!
I bet you do all kinds of right.

I'm afraid of losing my friends if I go to Japan for a year.
Well, you'll never lose me.
I know that we laughed after you said this, but Kayla it was so sweet! You'll never lose my friendship, either.♥

Sunday, April 11
Thesis countdown: 23 days, 20 comic pages remaining.
Talked to Dad about contracts. He gave me tips for writing counter-proposals.
Uh-huh. OK.
He also gave me his opinion about JET (again).
You'll have your whole life to travel. This is not travel. This is an intensive cultural immersion. Ask yourself how worthwhile that is, given your length of study with Japan already.
Walked to the grocery store and back for a little exercise and fresh air.
Called home and talked to the family.
We're in the middle of LOST!
Oooooh! Okay, no spoilers, but... IT'S THE BEST ONE OF THE SEASON!!

Monday, April 12

Thesis countdown: 22 days, 18 comic pages remaining.
inch

grin
wriggle
I love spring. It's so warm, I forget that I have Reynaud's.

Drew a page of Over the Surface start-to-finish in 6 hours. Didn't know I could work so quickly!
nice!
thanks!

My life right now is not boyfriend-friendly. I don't have time to treat you the way you deserve...!

Tuesday, April 13

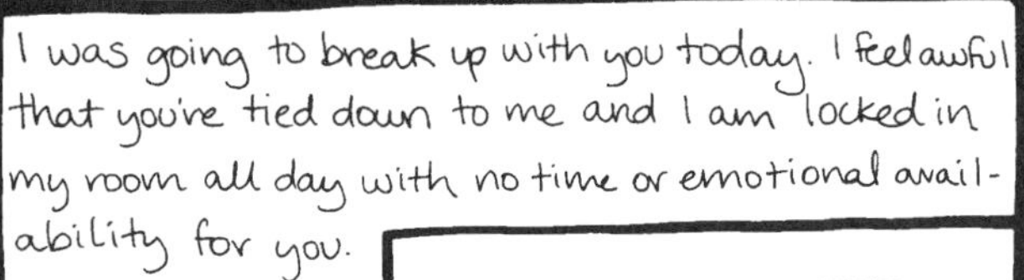
I was going to break up with you today. I feel awful that you're tied down to me and I am locked in my room all day with no time or emotional availability for you.

...

I don't want you to stress over me, though.
But, I feel bad.... You deserve someone who's really HERE for you.
Don't! I just wish you had more time, for your sake.
You're really special. I just can't help feeling that you deserve someone who returns your thoughtfulness more reliably.

But you spoke first:
I feel really bad that you feel crunched for time...

Was it the change in my mood that brought the sun out? It's suddenly smiling-at-strangers weather!

Watched Ohayo in JPN 307. TOOTS ADORBS! "I love you!" It reminds me of little Neil and how we would get him to say adult things. He could make anything cute!
Shall we shag now, or shall we shag later?

Wednesday, April 14

Yet another job opportunity popped up today! I am paralyzed by my options.
I see the best in every scenario...!

I feel like a skier, poised at the top of the mountain of possibilities. At the bottom are set career paths. I have to position myself very thoughtfully now because the further I get down any run I take, the harder it will be to change course. You may think that this is a ridiculous way to view the world, but everything seems very serious and permanent to me right now. Like I only have one chance to start.

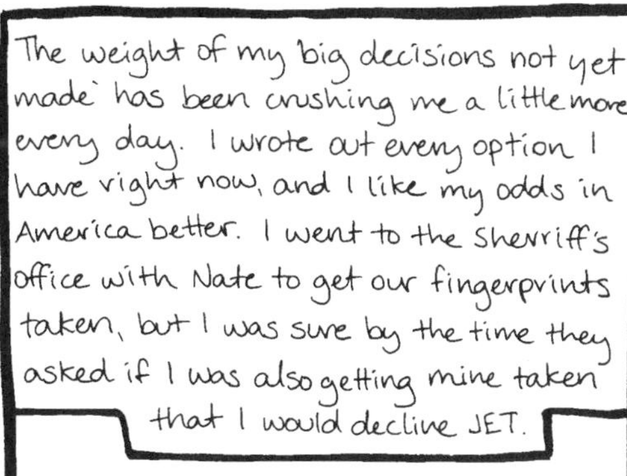
The weight of my big decisions not yet made has been crushing me a little more every day. I wrote out every option I have right now, and I like my odds in America better. I went to the Sherriff's office with Nate to get our fingerprints taken, but I was sure by the time they asked if I was also getting mine taken that I would decline JET.

No.

I slammed my head in the car door! HOW?!
!
That takes skill...

Can I be your 'failure to launch' daughter next year?

Impulsively, I went to Sakura's for California rolls at the end of the day. Suji was working and we talked when she was free.
It feels like I'm not eating alone.

Thursday, April 15
Mom asked why I decided not to do JET. I said because it would be too hard to say goodbye to people after making year-long friendships. She did NOT like that answer.
WORDS OF WISDOM FROM: MOM
If you live life afraid to connect with people because you don't want to say 'goodbye', you will shut yourself off from many things. You have to just let yourself get attached and be grateful for what you had together.
gulp
Hazlenut pirouettes yummmmmmmmmm
Watched UP with Nate.
I thought that you weren't interested in me.
I thought that you weren't interested in me!
We must both be shy, huh?
80s Night at Henry's
Are you drunk enough for this?
No.
No. Are you?
Want another drink?
Yeah.

Friday, April 16

no one home
open
within reach from window
Wrote 6 pages of thesis and drew 2 pages of comic! Win for productivity!
YAH!
I still just feel like crying. I know I am going to have regrets and wonder what could have been.
But every time I rethink the decision, I come to the same conclusion.
This is the right choice.
SUPER EMPOWERMENT SUNRISE!
CRASHING WAVES OF WILLPOWER!
SPRING!
HOKAY. Because I turned down that awesome option, I am going to get my butt in gear to make my situation next year THE BEST POSSIBLE. I am going to pursue my dreams like never before.

Saturday, April 17
Breakfast burritos at Siena w/ Hannah!
I can't eat anymoooooooore!
EAT IT
I did.
I'm going to throw up.
I'm really going to throw up.
Worked on our theses until the library closed.
sigh
Went to John Henry's to get my debit card back from Thursday night.
Buy you a drink while we're here?
Sure!
Then we got nachos at Rennie's!
I've totally seen people come in for just food before.
Oh good. I feel weird ....

Sunday, April 18

Writing my thesis and losing my mind. What am I trying to say in these 25 rambling pages?

Second Coffee, save me!
*

Wrote until 7:30 and called home.
Anything new with you?
I just finished my rough draft, but otherwise... no. It's thesis thesis thesis thesis times here.

Finished coloring a commission!
YUSS!

And finished another page of Over the Surface!
DOUBLE YUSS!!
Today was such a success!

Monday, April 19

I woke up with a headache that quickly morphed into a migraine. I only get them once or twice a year and they are always horrible and humbling.
Oh no....

Basically, I writhe in pain under my covers trying to block out all light and fall asleep (even a short sleep usually ends the migraine)...

...But every hour or so the pain makes me vomit.

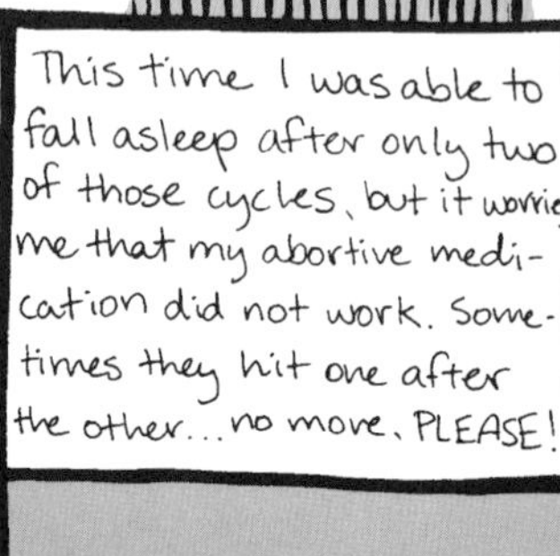

This time I was able to fall asleep after only two of those cycles, but it worries me that my abortive medication did not work. Sometimes they hit one after the other... no more, PLEASE!

Read Snakes and Earrings in a single sitting. EEEEK!!

Tuesday, April 20

Delivered my first thesis draft to Alisa and Ben. Panic! I think the paper sucks right now, but I need their feedback at this stage, so I sucked it up and let them see what I have.
gulp
send!

Went to coffee with Nate between his classes.
It was our 3 month earlier this week!
Wow! I thought we were coming up on a land-mark...
Oh god, I'm awful. I'm an awful person. Should I have been counting? What is he counting from...?

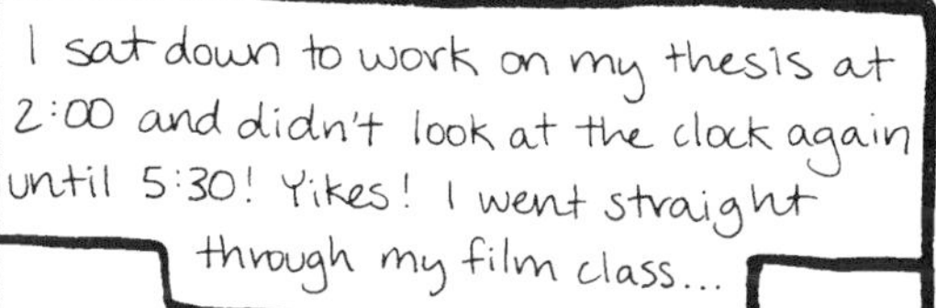
I sat down to work on my thesis at 2:00 and didn't look at the clock again until 5:30! Yikes! I went straight through my film class...

fwip

Drew one and a half pages of Over the Surface. 14 days until I turn it in.
I think that we're

Wednesday, April 21

I love graffiti. When it is well-designed and on an otherwise ugly wall, I think it is such an improvement. I love the anonymous nature of it as well. I take pictures of a lot of graffiti around Eugene and keep track of where I have seen certain designs. In another life, I would love to be a graffiti artist.
The quiz in JPN 307 didn't necessitate seeing the movie last night! So lucky!!
Hmm, well, I forgot my Powerpoint, so.... Tell me your favorite and least favorite parts about the film!
YAAAY!
Penciled 2 pages of Over the Surface and inked 3. 13 days left....!

Thursday, April 22

So many little things I have to remember to do today... it's like holding onto sand! You're just not going to get it all.

twitter
140

Burned Nate an Andrew Bird CD he wanted. I tried to make a watercolor sketch to accompany it, but it sucks!

CRUMPLE

Sat on the other side of the classroom in JPN 410 and finally got to talk to this really interesting person who is into comics, too.

TARGET
FRIEND

Went to the bank for cash to use at Stumptown.

CASH DANCE

CASH DANCE

Haircut! I look like I did when I was 9 years old.

pat

Patting my bob haughtily was one of my little kid tricks that I knew made adults laugh.

Friday, April 23

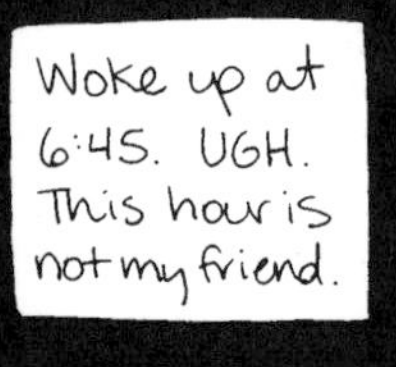
Woke up at 6:45. UGH. This hour is not my friend.

Put on my new sheath dress. I'll take even the slightest excuse to dress up!

Caught a 9:00 train to Portland and spent my time working through contract legalese. It feels very dicey, like a small mistake now could be very harmful later.

Watched What Not to Wear with Mom.
WNTW

DRINK 'N' DRAW LIKE A LADY!! I was really nervous and excited that I got to meet Hope Larson, Kate Beaton, and Lucy Knisley. Also, talking with ladies who are just getting started in comics was great; I still get nervous walking into a room of comic folks, so props to the newbies who came!

Went to O'Brien's for a nightcap with Emi, Joëlle, Nico, Jamie, and Jamie's friend Bobby. I got the last order of fries from the kitchen ☺

HEY-O

Saturday, April 24

STUMPTOWN!!!!

I tabled with Emi and Angie ♡

I met Emi's friend Lindsay. What a sweetheart!

I came back to the table and saw Kurt Busiek browsing my minis! WHAT? He bought Over the Surface!

?
OMIGOD AWESOME

Oh my god comics. Mercury, Dar volume 2, French Milk, Spellcheckers, Hark a Vagrant, sketches, prints, and more!

Exciting conversations go like this:

We should talk.

!!!

ANY. TIME.

After-afterparty at Brett Warnock's!

You've gotta read this...
DA-YUM
and this
and this
and this...

We finally went home at 2.

THANKS, BRETT!!
I'm never going to finish my thesis...

Sunday, April 25

Let myself sleep in, rolled into the con 15 minutes before it started.

ooog

Mom, Aunt Karin, and Uncle Dave came by and said
Hi!

Ben and Alisa both came by the table this weekend. It feels really, really good, seeing my primary and secondary thesis advisors at the con – like I picked the right people.

Seriously, Stumptown is so great. Everybody is legitimately interested in comics and art, and they'll come up and have a conversation about it with no ulterior motive. I love just talking tools and influences with random people sometimes!

Went home right after the con and watched Avatar with the family for Family Night.
Me-ow!
DAAAD!!

Monday, April 26
Convention hangover. My brain is dead and time flies by. I have a lot to do today, damnit!
Is there a gentle way to break up with someone?
Do it in public.
Nick
Private. Definitely private.
Mom
Just ignore him. Don't respond to his texts.
Be honest. Tell him the truth.
I wanna make it right, that is the way, to turn my life around, today is the day
Natalie, it was maddening, the way you lead me on and on. Even when you were here, you were already gone
I could say that I'll always have feelings for you, but I've got a life ahead of me and I'm only 22
I know exactly where I'm going; I'm getting closer and closer every day and I'm almost there, I'm almost there. People down here think I'm crazy, but I don't care.

Tuesday, April 27

I don't set an alarm anymore because my body wakes me up between 8 and 9AM every day, but today I woke up at 11:30! ACK!
I want you to have fun spring term of your senior year, and I don't want to feel guilty for putting all of my energy into comics. I'm sorry for guilting you about the voicemail message... I wanted an excuse, but it was nothing.
Weird weather this week. It's sunny but cold, so I wear sunglasses and 2 coats.
YOU LOOK RIDICULOUS
Had a small panic attack in Professor Freedman's office as we talked about my thesis (due in 7 days!!).
It needs some major changes...
More jobs rolling in from Stumptown! Wonderful! I can't take anything new on until my thesis presentation is over; hope they'll still be interested...
I have a heavy heart from the breakup.
It feels right, but it doesn't feel good.

Wednesday, April 28

Woke up early and started drawing. Finished the Holly Golightly commission and 3 Over the Surface pages. Phenomenal! I'm still fighting to meet my deadlines, but today helped.

Went to the library to work on my thesis. Ate a granola bar for dinner. Very depressing.

Loud people in the library infuriate me. Headphones as loud as I can stand, but I can still hear them! Makes me want to...
HULK OUT

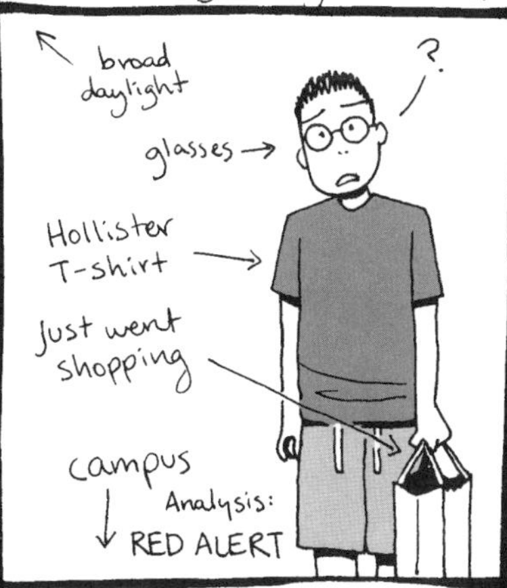
I get nervous when strangers try to talk to me. Even when it's someone totally harmless like an exchange student looking for Pegasus Pizza.
broad daylight
?
glasses
Hollister T-shirt
Just went shopping
campus
Analysis: RED ALERT
In some ways, I am still a 7 year old, and I might always be.

Total thesis paralysis. I wanted to pass with distinction, but now even passing sounds good...

Thursday, April 29

I've had recurring nightmares....

I was loved for who I am and missed the opportunity to be a better man

You just need to take this skinny, self-deprecating pony of a paper and turn it into a fat, confident pony.

Everyone is trying to make eye contact with me today. What? Is it the weather? Do I seem sad? Do you like my legs?
WHAT?!

I penciled and inked 4½ pages today, even with 2 classes. Who am I?! I hope I like them when I look at them in a week, but I am so proud of my newfound speed.

Friday, April 30

Can barely get out of bed.

Watched a fellow HC student defend her thesis and pass with honors. Very good for my nerves to watch someone else defend.

4:00 PM

Let's dance, thesis.

3:15 AM

OH YEAH

WHO'S BAD!?

Saturday, May 1
It's a short thesis respite while Alisa has my paper.
Aaaaaah.
I slept until noon, showered, and did my hair and makeup.
Went to the grocery store, only to find that my debit card expired! Nooooooo!
NO FOOD FOR YOU.
I've been thinking....maybe I could use Kickstarter to raise funds to self-pubish Between Gears once the art is all done...
tap tap
You think that could work...?
I'm gonna need to buy earplugs again. It felt like I was periodically woken up every hour from 12-6 AM. Note to self: do not live in party central.
RRRRRRR...

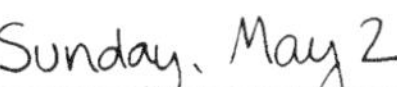
Sunday, May 2

Finished the art for Over the Surface 2! WHOOOO!

Donesies!

flourish

Talked with the family:

What are you going to do now that you don't have a boy-friend?

PFFFF, what?!!

Uhhh... hang out with my friends, do some art projects, and live in a neater house?

It might sound sad, but I really haven't noticed the absence, because I didn't have time to hang out with him before. Now I just don't feel guilty when I'm working.

That *is* sad.

Nate was a really wonderful boyfriend, but at this point in my life, I don't take relationships seriously and I'm happy to get back to having 'me' time and no responsibility to another person. My friends say I'm a total boy when it comes to love.

Okay with that

Went to the library to print Over the Surface 2 prototypes. I am so happy with them! There are corrections to make, of course, and things I can do better next time, but I am proud of the comic.

Yaaay!! ♡

Monday, May 3
Met with Professor Southworth, the 3rd leg of my thesis committee, today for the first time in 2 months. It was a huge relief to hear her say:
This looks great. I think it will be a matter next week of deciding whether you pass with honors or distinction.
I made it my goal to pass with distinction when I saw Heather do it last year. Only the top 10-15% of HC theses pass with distinction. I would be soooooo happy if I did it!
Things I Hate: Getting stuck behind a smoker on the sidewalk.
Ordered a new debit card at the bank. I paid for groceries today in $1 bills from Stumptown. I would rather not do that again.
Would you believe me if I told you that I'm not a stripper?
Ha ha
I just hit a big savings goal! I want to have several months' savings built up in addition to a sustainable income before I move out of my parents' house in the fall. I am about 2/3 of the way there!

Tuesday, May 4

We did the wall sit in pilates today for 3 minutes. To pass the time, Dana and I told jokes.

How many hipsters does it take to screw in a lightbulb?

Oh, you haven't heard of the number.

How many feminists does it take to screw in a lightbulb?

That's NOT funny.

How many emo kids does it take to screw in a lightbulb?

COMB

YOU DON'T UNDERSTAND!

How many Vietnam war vets does it take to screw in a lightbulb?

YOU DON'T KNOW! YOU WEREN'T THERE!!

I feel like I'm at the top of a mountain, looking down at what I conquered..

My thesis...

Classes...

Conventions...

Big decisions about next year...

I feel really good about this.

It was rough, but I held it all together.

Wednesday, May 5
AAAAAAA
POW
Thesis SENT! Now I have 1 week to prepare the 20-minute presentation for my defense next Wednesday.

LOST made me cry. Whimpering, moaning, blubbering crying.
WHY?!
WHYYYYY?!!!

I didn't make the connection between Cinco de Mayo and turning in my thesis until Hannah called and asked,

Rennie's, 11:00?

DA♥HA!

Hannah's irresistable sexual magnetism got us free drinks!!

Heeeeeeey!

THANKS, DUDE!!

. . .

SMACK

You realize that to find our new nacho-serving bar in Portland, we're going to have to try all of them?

I am fully aware.

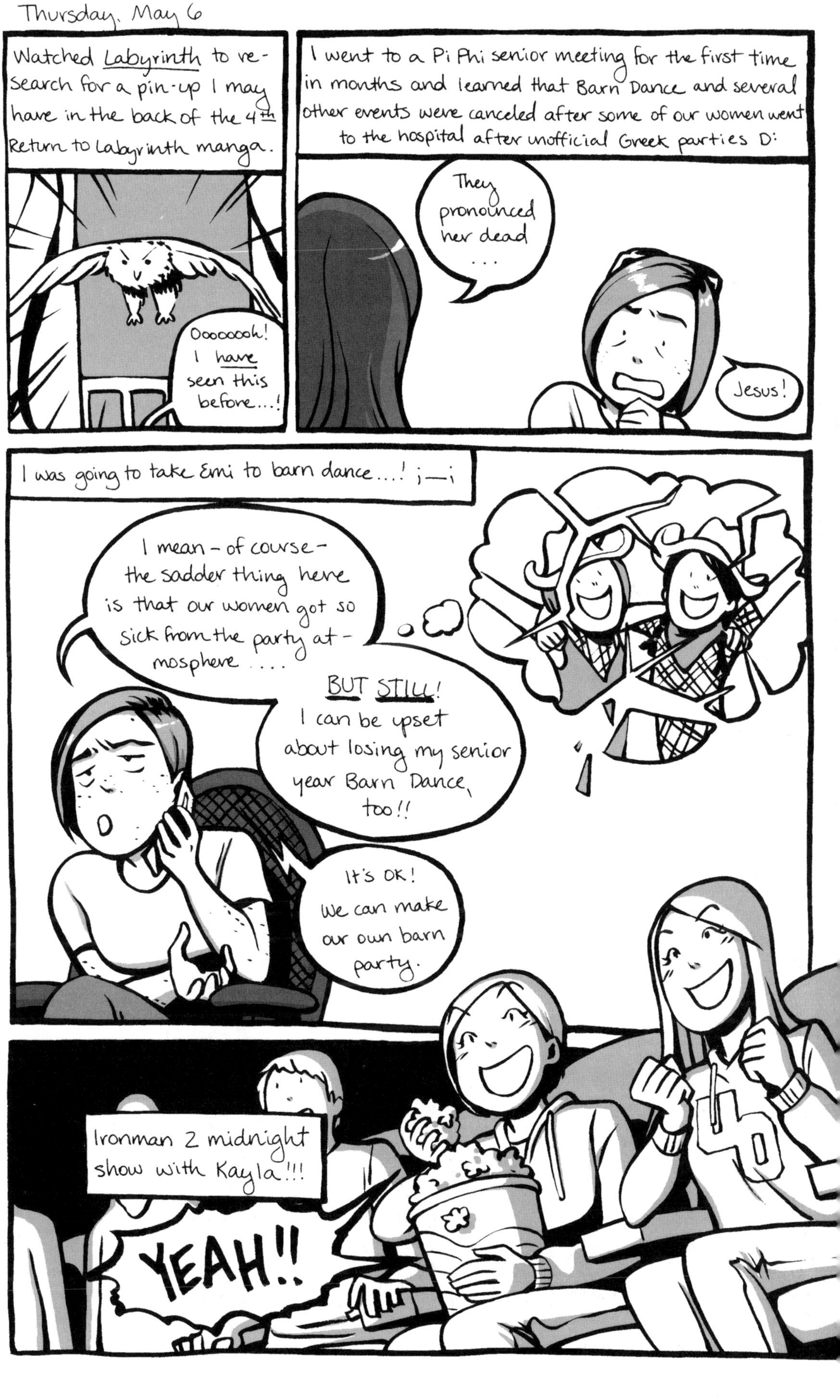

Thursday, May 6

Watched Labyrinth to research for a pin-up I may have in the back of the 4th Return to Labyrinth manga.

Oooooooh! I have seen this before...!

I went to a Pi Phi senior meeting for the first time in months and learned that Barn Dance and several other events were canceled after some of our women went to the hospital after unofficial Greek parties D:

They pronounced her dead ...
Jesus!

I was going to take Emi to barn dance...! ;—;

I mean — of course — the sadder thing here is that our women got so sick from the party atmosphere ....

BUT STILL! I can be upset about losing my senior year Barn Dance, too!!

It's OK! We can make our own barn party.

Ironman 2 midnight show with Kayla!!!

YEAH!!

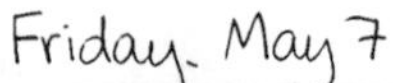
Friday. May 7

SLAM
SLAM
SLAM
I am so sick of living in this pig sty. 5 more weeks and then never again.

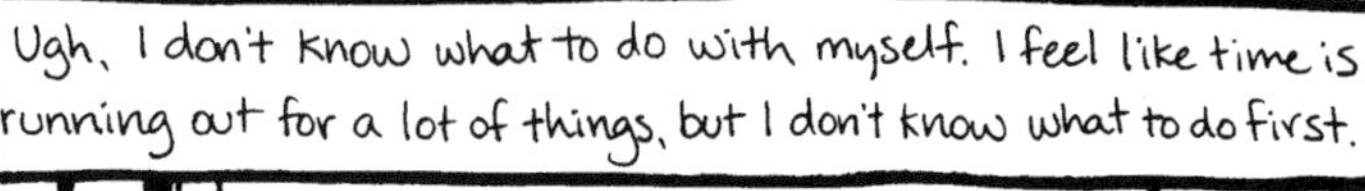
Ugh, I don't know what to do with myself. I feel like time is running out for a lot of things, but I don't know what to do first.

Talked with Emi a lot online today. Can't wait to talk in person this summer!

Napped off and on in the evening. Kept feeling like I was about to fall off of a cliff and stopping myself at the last second.
When I didn't stop was when I fell asleep.

Saturday, May 8

WOOOOAAHHH!!

Woke up to awesome Over the Surface fan art from Nico! Gotta do some better Spell Checkers fan art....

Made a fan mix for Snakes + Earrings for my JPN 410 mid-term. Best class everrrrr!

Snakes + Earrings fan mix

Did that Spell Checkers fan art :P Those girls are nasty, but boy howdy they are fun to draw.

What're you looking at, Plebe?

....

Emi called and we chatted for an hour! It was wonderful to catch up and dream about next year.
And we'll have another cartoonist on hand any time we need advice!
Aww, like a mini Periscope!

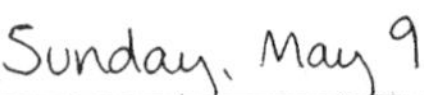
Sunday, May 9

cleaned house for house tours. For the love of God, someone sign the lease for next year! I don't wanna waste any more days on giving house tours!
Come on in...

Happy Mothers Day! ♡

Day 9 without a debit card: I scrounged for change to go grocery shopping.
Ooh! A quarter!

I sat next to Niha in the library and neither of us realized for 5 minutes. We are both furiously working on our theses, but still. Awareness fail!

Dear Safeway Checkout Boy, you are a saint. Even though I got into the Express Lane with 12 items... and ended up putting 3 of them back because I didn't have enough quarters to pay for everything....
I'M SORRY
It's OK!

And left my house keys at the counter.... you just smiled and said,
Thank youuu...
No problem.

Monday, May 10

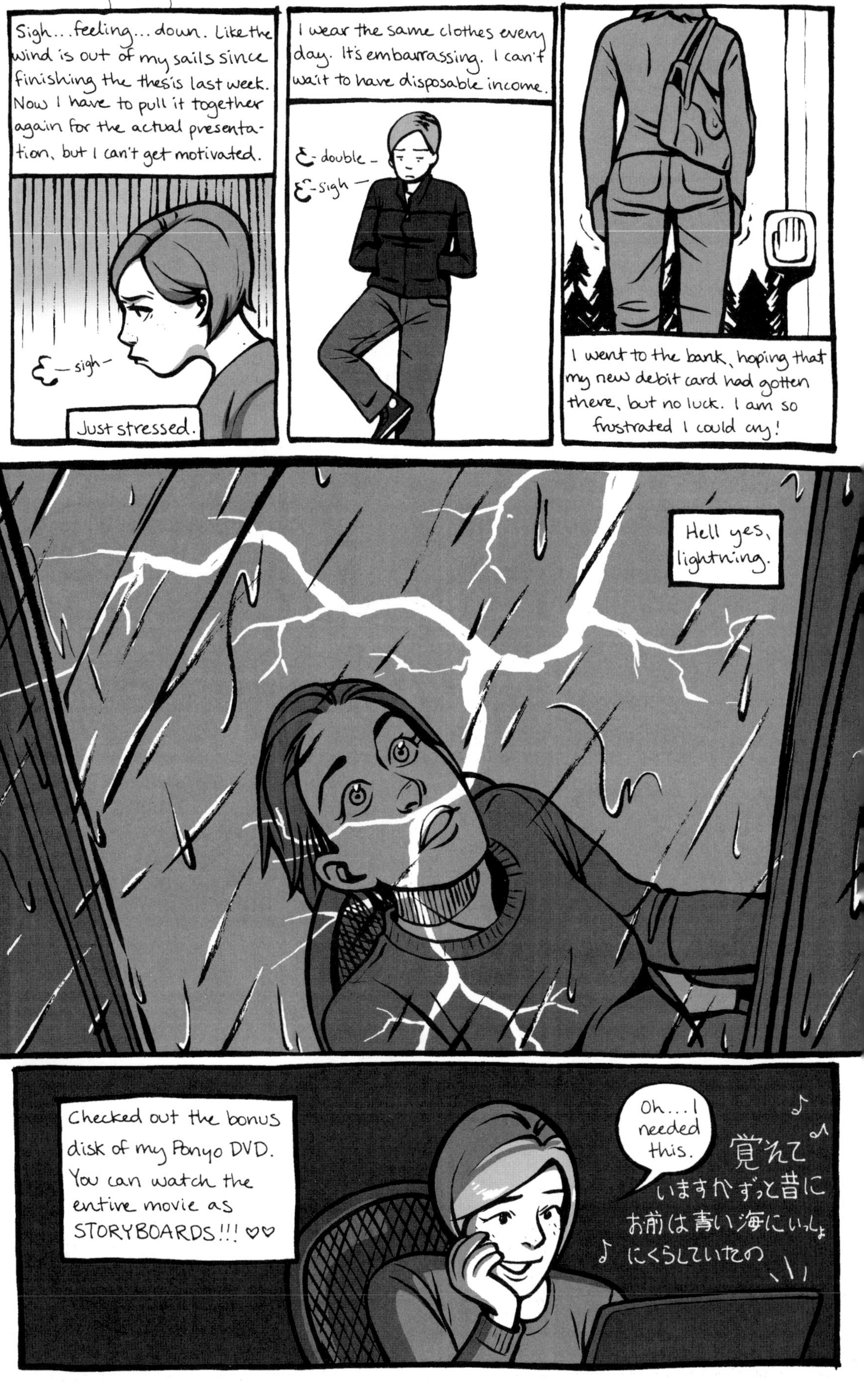

Sigh... feeling... down. Like the wind is out of my sails since finishing the thesis last week. Now I have to pull it together again for the actual presentation, but I can't get motivated.

—sigh—
Just stressed.

I wear the same clothes every day. It's embarrassing. I can't wait to have disposable income.
—double—
—sigh—

I went to the bank, hoping that my new debit card had gotten there, but no luck. I am so frustrated I could cry!

Hell yes, lightning.

Checked out the bonus disk of my Ponyo DVD. You can watch the entire movie as STORYBOARDS!!! ♡♡
Oh... I needed this.
♪ 覚えていますか ずっと昔に お前は青い海にいっしょにくらしていたの ♪

Friday, May 21

Closest I have ever felt to vomiting from drinking. I am normally very rational, but I'm disappointed in my failure to say 'no' to that 3rd drink. (HEY, they were STRONG.)

FAIL morning. DDD: I left my debit card at John Henry's again!!! How the hell am I going to get it back?! Left the kettle on when I left the house, had to run back, was almost late for Nate's thesis presentation
ARE YOU KIDDING ME?!!

Answered e-mails for 4 hours. Oh, that screen on my eyes!
目がー!
目がー!!

*Hella nerd points if you can identify the Ghibli reference

Things are gooooood!! Reading a revised contract from one publisher and e-mailing with another! So excited about both!

Called a taxi to take me to the bar and back for my debit card. Got a cool driver who told me how he knows when people are going to ditch the fee and how to avoid it.
A lot of cab drivers become writers because of all of the weird stories they accumulate.
Hmm... I do need a part-time job this summer ...
I would love a day job that exposed me to an array of people the way that cab driving would, but I need regular daytime hours.

Wednesday, May 12

I hour before I present my thesis......

Oh god oh god, I am going to throw up...!

BREATHE

OH GOD

I was so nervous that the whole thing is just a blur in my memory. I didn't even get to my last 3 slides!

But I guess I did well, because....

We have decided to pass you with distinction.

☆☆☆☆☆

"Top 2%"! I can't get that part out of my head!

I am deliriously happy...!

Good. You should allow yourself to be for a while.

Everything feels right. Like it's the end of the year in a Harry Potter book, Gryffindor won the house cup, and every thing is falling into place better than you could have even hoped.

LET THE WILD RUMPUS START!!

Celebratory drinking at Rennies with Hannah and Danielle.

What's one story you're not going to tell your daughter?

Oh ho ho...

Thursday, May 13

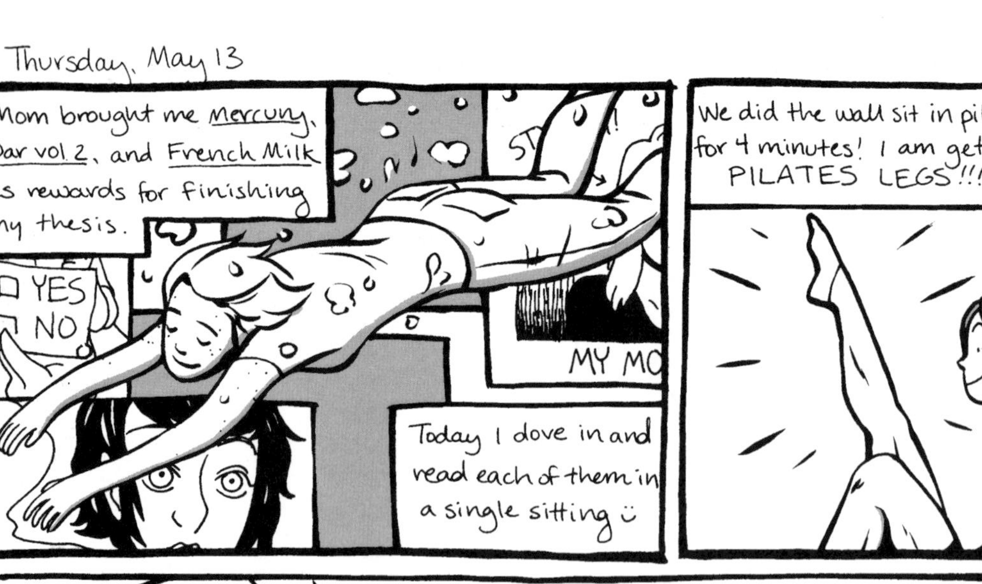

Mom brought me Mercury, Dar vol. 2, and French Milk as rewards for finishing my thesis.
YES
NO
MY MO
Today I dove in and read each of them in a single sitting ☺
We did the wall sit in pilates for 4 minutes! I am getting PILATES LEGS!!! ☺

I thought about how nice it would be to have a partner... someone who is always there to share my success and have inside jokes with and just... rely on. Always. I guess I'm getting closer to understanding the term 'life partner' and why it's worth looking for one.

Clark Honors College Dinner Dance! The timing with my thesis could not have been more perfect. And the wine flowed ~~~

OK, I'm drunk and this is cheesy, but...

I am so happy to know you guys! You are actually going to make a difference in the world and I am going to be so proud to say that I went to college with you!!

Umm, same for YOU!

Drunk talk in the bathroom with Hannah+Christina!

Friday, May 14
Wow, I have Friday, Saturday, Sunday, and Monday with no classes and no big stressful projects. Unbelievable.
I can do anything!
Catching up on the art projects I had to delay for the thesis.
Also had an idea for a new short story!
"Give me your Pi Social money!"
Give me a suitable replacement for Barn Dance.
Went to the new Eugene location of Voodoo Donuts with Hannah and Danielle, but they sold out hours ago.
CLOSED

Saturday, May 15

Wrote out all of my hopes and goals for next year. It has the potential to be a wonderful life.

Gotta work hard and be frugal, but living in Portland with my family and friends and the comic community, getting opportunities to work as an artist... it's a really good start.

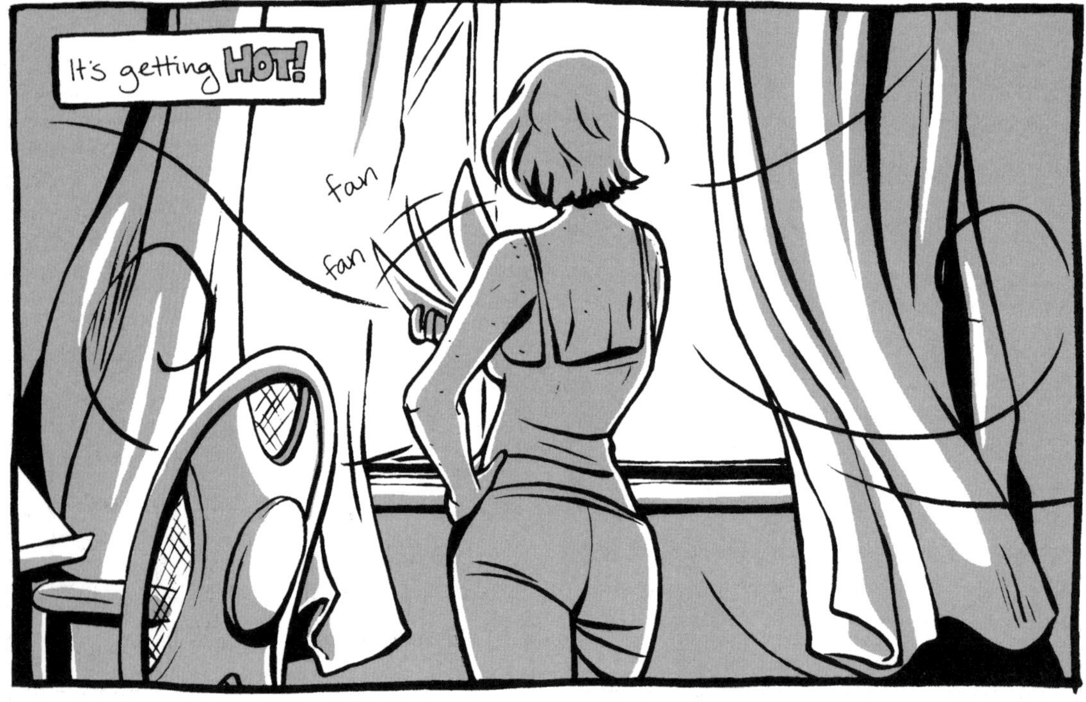

It's getting HOT!
fan
fan

Sunday, May 16

Ducklings in the mill race!

Mom asked me something on Wednesday that I have been thinking about ever since:
Is there anyone you'll be sad to leave college without dating?
....

The answer is:
YES!

There are at least a dozen! People I just assumed I would date sooner or later, probably when we found ourselves in a class together or something, but it never happened.

I'm not sad to leave college without dating them, though. It never worked in college for a reason, and not having a dating history with them leaves things open for the future if we ever find ourselves thrown into the same sphere again and hit it off. By not dating them in college, I feel like I left future me a bunch of possible surprise presents.

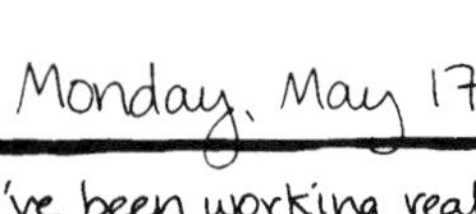
Monday, May 17

I've been working really hard on improving my art between Over the Surface and my next big project. Today, I looked at tons of talented artists' work and started to get really down on myself for not drawing as well as they do.

Why can't I ink like that?

Why can't I lay out my pages like that?

Why can't I draw clothes like that?

But I reminded myself: you can't be everything! Even these artists that I love have weak areas. I was subconsciously combining the best parts of each of them into Talent Mecha and comparing myself to that.

I will not hold myself to the standard of Talent Mecha... Talent Mecha does not exist...

I can still learn a lot from each of them, but I need to cut myself some slack.

Finished the first page for my short story in the Less Than Three anthology.

My own script is making me blush....

Shipped 4 Etsy orders and recieved 2 more today! Yippee!
This is actually becoming profitable!
I have to remember to save money for taxes on these sales, though...

Tuesday, May 18

Least favorite pilates pose:

SIDE PLANK

We talked about publishing and copyrights today in JPN 410, and one of my classmates told this horror story about a comic artist who lost her copyright to her PRINTER when she self-published!
Terrifying!
!
Mental note: read all contracts thoroughly!
Homework is so hard in these final weeks...!!
I wrote a 38-page paper and drew 20 comic pages last month...
...This is a 1-page paper, and I don't think I can get through it!

Because I resisted buying sushi last night when I craved it, I spent $10 on things I wanted at Safeway.

Wednesday, May 19

Got sushi today. Fiscal responsi-bility fail. Unagi+katsu bowl win.

I realized something: once school is over, there will be something else stressing us out... growing up, getting a job... once that stress is over, we'll stress about finding boyfriends, getting married, maybe having kids...

Yeah. I think that life is never constant—we'll always be in transition or adjusting to a change.

Favorite things:

Wind so strong that tree trunks sway. It reminds me that even they bend.

Reflections in puddles moving with you as you walk alongside them.

Helped Hannah practice for her thesis presentation.

I did it for my stuffed animals.

They don't give you feedback.

That was my problem.

After the thesis practice and wine, we found that we both still remember every word of the Pokemon theme song.

I WANNA BE THE VERY BEST

LIKE NO ONE EVER WAS!

Thursday, May 20
Hannah's thesis presentation! To loosen her up, we played the Pokemon theme song on the fancy projector in her nice room before everyone got there.
I KNOW IT'S MY
DESTINY~~!
WORDS OF WISDOM
FROM: MY DOVE CHOCOLATE
"Blessings only come to those who notice."
I think that's the best one yet.
80's Night at John Henry's to celebrate Hannah's defense!
Do you regret it?
NO.
Then you did the right thing.
shake

Friday, May 21

Closest I have ever felt to vomiting from drinking. I am normally very rational, but I'm disappointed in my failure to say 'no' to that 3rd drink. (HEY, they were STRONG.)

FAIL morning. DDD: I left my debit card at John Henry's again!!! How the hell am I going to get it back?! Left the kettle on when I left the house, had to run back, was almost late for Nate's thesis presentation.
ARE YOU KIDDING ME?!!

Answered e-mails for 4 hours. Oh, that screen on my eyes!
目がー! 目がー!!
*Hella nerd points if you can identify the Ghibli reference

Things are goooooood!! Reading a revised contract from one publisher and e-mailing with another! So excited about both!

Called a taxi to take me to the bar and back for my debit card. Got a cool driver who told me how he knows when people are going to ditch the fee and how to avoid it.

A lot of cab drivers become writers because of all of the weird stories they accumulate.
Hmm... I do need a part-time job this summer ....

I would love a day job that exposed me to an array of people the way that cab driving would, but I need regular daytime hours.

Saturday, May 22
Bought regalia. It cost me all but the last of my checking accaunt ;;
Last reviews of the contract from Lerner. Looks pretty good to me!
It's just about signing time~!
Imagine a hell where you are doing sit-ups. Your body is exhausted, your musles aching, but you can't make your body stop doing sit-ups.
Menstrual cramps. That hell is called menstrual cramps.
Emi called and we talked for an hour and a half :D
I love when we both cover the same thing in Emitown and Between Gears.
I know! I love seeing which part of the conversation you remember or think is important.
HA HA. 'Which part I remember.'
You know what I mean.

Sunday, May 23

How the hell is it still so cold at night that I can't sleep in sweats, socks, and my North Face hoodie?! It's May! Even in Oregon, it should be really warm by now!
CH-CH-CH-C

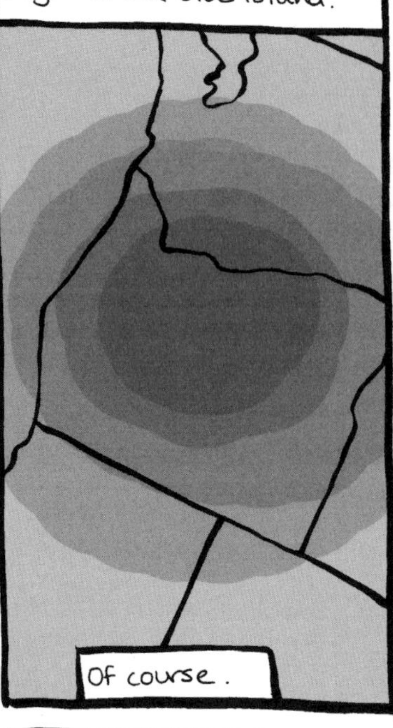
I once saw a global climate model's prediction about which regions will get warmer and colder over time. In a sea of red increasing temperatures, Oregon was a blue island.
Of course.

Lazy day. Woke up late, didn't shower, didn't leave the house.

Oooooh man... I can't wait to get out of here. 23 more days in Eugene. In this house. In this lifestyle. I need a change, and a big one is drawing near.

Stayed off of the internet after the LOST series finale started on the east coast.
Do not want spoilers!!

Wore my retainers for the first time in several months.
OW!

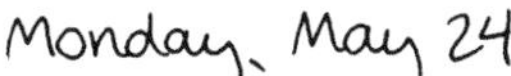
Monday, May 24

I was good and did 6 class readings and 2 forum posts before doing any art today!

All of my shows have ended their seasons, and the timing is oddly appropriate in the context of my life right now.

Watched the LOST series finale.

sniff!

We are approaching the time of 'lasts'. Tonight was my last Pi Phi chapter.
It was happy/sad, like most endings.

Mom and Dad wrote a 'senior spotlight' for me.
"We're so proud of all you've accomplished and who you've grown into..."
N'aww, Mom and Dad. :)

Tuesday, May 25
Waiting for the HC elevator, I danced like no one was watching.
oh I'm just a girl, living in captivity
...But someone was.
snk
Picked up my tickets for graduation. PHEW!
GET!
Finalizing plans with Mom for our San Fran grad road trip! So exciting!
blah.. .Redwoods... ...shopping.. ..wine...
nod!
Watched Cruel Story of Youth in JPN307.
I want those two hours back.
That movie was so bad I need to go take a shower.
I think I am sick for the first time since my tonsillectomy. You may laugh, but I just have to see that as a wonderful thing! 5 months without getting sick? That would have been impossible for me last year. I didn't know that I had a problem, but looking back, I was sick all the time. My life is totally different now, not losing all of those days to illness.
AH~
K-X-PH!!!

Wednesday, May 26

I try to smile at strangers on the street, but a defense mechanism that sets in when I am the least bit self-conscious is my street face....a scary thing.

Sometimes I blow right by people I know and they have to grab my shoulder and say my name for me to snap out of it.

Oh!
Hi!

The sudden change must be funny to people watching.

20 days. And boy, am I counting.
drum
drum
drum
drum
drum

You know, I'm doing alright on those 2010 goals:

1. Make a GREAT thesis — check!
2. Graduate —— on track
3. Have fun and sell stuff at ECCC and Stumptown —— check!
4. Finish Between Gears —— on track
5. Start my next big comic — scheduled
6. Get a JOB! —— scheduled

Instead of my usual nighttime munchies (popcorn, cereal), I scrambled an egg with mushrooms. Sooo good! I really want to learn to cook better and put in the time next year to eat well. :)

Thursday, May 27
I thought that the big spider on the ceiling of our bath-room was scary, but I like it even less when it's not there.
glance
glance
SUMMER GOALS
① Consolidate belongings, get rid of a LOT of stuff.
② Save money for at least 3 months' expenses (about $3500?)
③ Secure a sustainable monthly income
④ Spend time with Mom, Dad, Nick, Neil, sketch group, comic/high school/college/family friends
⑤ Move in with Emi before the weather turns bad (September? October?)
⑥ Read books!!! At least 3 purely for fun, please
Sniiiiiiiiiiiiiiiiiiiiiiiiff
My sinuses.........owww.

Friday, May 28

Did my last homework assignment today! Wrote my last paper for JPN 307.

DONE

Watched ANTM cycle 14, which gave me MAKEOVER FEVER.

MUST CUT!
MUST COLOR!
MUST BUY...!

My wardrobe has become very sad in the 3 years I haven't had a job. I don't expect to be rolling in dough any time soon, but next year I should have enough money to at least go shopping once in a while.

hmm...
flick

I think my favorite look right now is just skinny jeans, ballet flats, a t-shirt, scarf, and a jacket. Simple, practical, chic ♡

And I want to keep my hair its natural color and grow it out at one length.

And wear red lipstick!!

AND EYELINER!!!! :D

Saturday, May 29

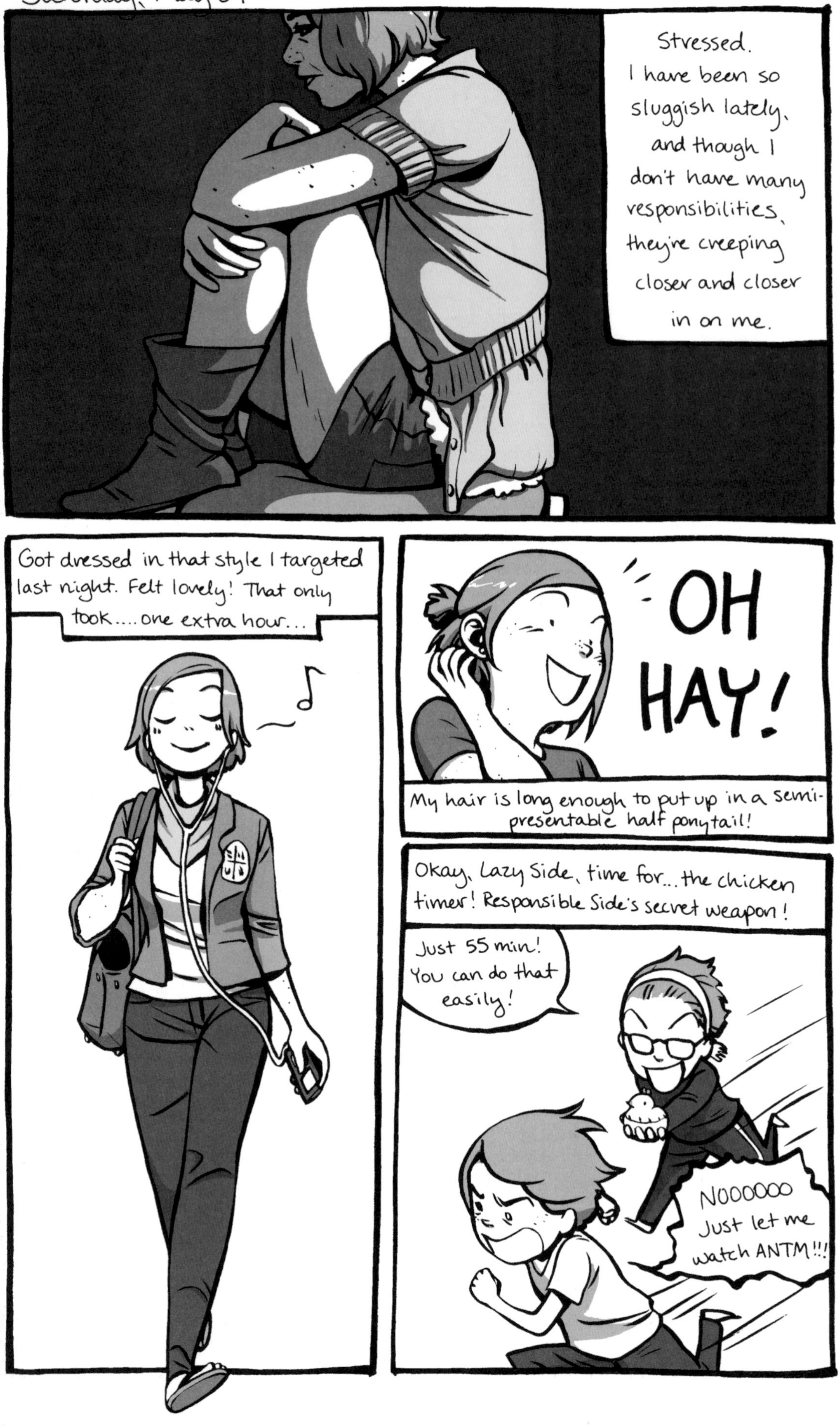

Stressed. I have been so sluggish lately, and though I don't have many responsibilities, they're creeping closer and closer in on me.

Got dressed in that style I targeted last night. Felt lovely! That only took.... one extra hour...

OH HAY!

My hair is long enough to put up in a semi-presentable half ponytail!

Okay, Lazy Side, time for... the chicken timer! Responsible Side's secret weapon!

Just 55 min! You can do that easily!

NOOOOOO Just let me watch ANTM!!!

Sunday, May 30

What happens when Niha leaves for the weekend? I sit araund belching in my underwear.
So cute.
Read up on the dangers of eating microwaved food. Gotta get off of my frozen dinner dependence next year....
Drew for hoooooooours. Very productive, very good art day.
Check,
check,
check!
Oh
my
GOD
AHA
HA
HA
HAHA
flail
HA
HA
flail
I GRADUATE
IN TWO WEEKS

Monday, May 31

My hand is dead from all of the drawing yesterday.
I had plans for you, but you need to rest today, huh?
nod

Snowy came up to me in the alley!!♡
Ohhh, thank you!♡
FOOD 65%
SLEEP 70%
CAT AFFECTION 100%

Met Ariston in the dorms, got my Scott Pilgrim 1-4 books back.
SCOTT PILGRIM'S

Got an e-mail from Imaoka Sensei at Jesuit. The school is phasing out Japanese! ;_; It feels like my childhood house is being torn down. Isn't Japanese still relevant enough to be taught in high school? What the heck are they replacing it with?!

Went to lunch at Carson with Lauren and Ariston, caught up, and had a great time. Our lives are uncertain, but Ariston is working in Japan this summer, Lauren is going into the Peace Corp, and I am going to draw graphic novels. We're pretty exciting, collectively!

Tuesday, June 1

Fitness test in pilates! I did the wall sit for 7 MINUTES!!

Now my body is trembley and noodley...

Last final test! JPN 307 is over!!!!!!!! :D

Overstimulation! @__@ Everything speeds up exponentially as the term comes to an end, but that effect is even worse spring term, especially senior year! Everyone wants to make plans and see each other, yet we are also busy with making arrangements to move out, get jobs, etc.
yeah, bye!
I'll call you!
I think I can, but I have these other two parties...
No, we will!
Totally, just let me know.
Don't leave before we
out agai

Went to Kinko's late at night.... long, rainy walk. I had to start the print job for my thesis, and I wanted to do it in person for quality assurance. It needs to be on cotton-y archival paper, etc.... No mess-ups!!

Wednesday, June 2

I would like nothing more than to take a day of physical rest, but I have errands.

Walked to Kinko's AGAIN in the rain. Got inside and it was humid and HOT, so I took off my jacket. Note: wearing a tank top will NOT get you service faster. It will just make 3 different guys tell you how long the wait is going to be.

Went to Professor Freedman's office to get her signature on my archival thesis copies. Talked with Nate outside of her office for a while.

Alisa always bakes cookies for her students on the last day of class. Even huge lecture classes!

I once had a seminar with 450 people...
wow!

I don't know how she does it, but it's a wonderful way to end the term.

Rewatched a movie from my childhood: Samson and Sally. It was much more disjointed and melancholy than I remembered. The movie has no solution to man's negative impact on the ocean — it just demonizes humans and shows how 2 whales live to adulthood. Realistic, but dark.

I'm suffocating!!

It's hard to even think about the BP oil spill. I avoid it because it makes me so sad and angry. I stumbled onto a news story today showing gorey pictures of dead whales and dolphins, and it just makes me cry to think that it's going on right now and I'm not stopping it and how could I stop it?

Thursday, June 3

What time is it??

SUMMER TIME!

Last day of class. Pilates, then JPN 410. Good way to end college classes. ♡

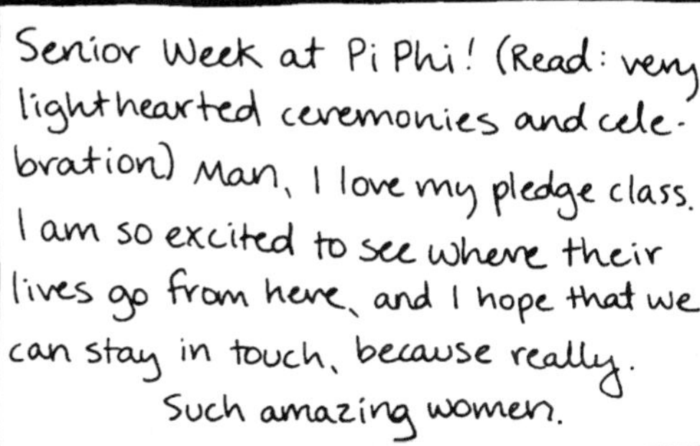
Senior Week at Pi Phi! (Read: very lighthearted ceremonies and celebration) Man, I love my pledge class. I am so excited to see where their lives go from here, and I hope that we can stay in touch, because really. Such amazing women.

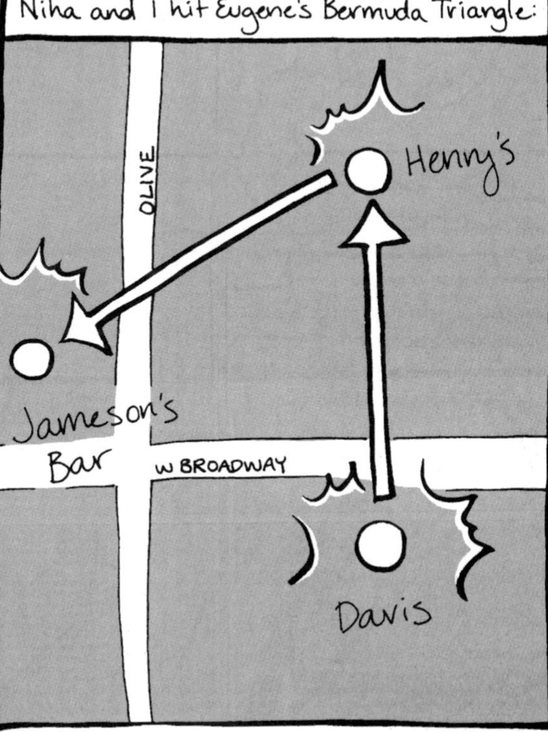
Niha and I hit Eugene's 'Bermuda Triangle':
OLIVE
Henry's
Jameson's Bar
W BROADWAY
Davis

DRUNK DRUNK DRUNK. All it took was 1 gin and tonic (and the vodka we prefunked with... but not much!), and I was gone.

Friday, June 4

Researched CLAMP's studio set-up and business model. They're pretty awesome. I wouldn't mind having a sweet place like that for PrADA.....

Cat café!!!

Bar

Porch ♡

Gallery

Tunnel System

BR

Regular café

End of Senior Week: dinner at Turtles. We recounted our favorite Pi Phi memories.
It's been quite a ride.
Oh, I forgot about that!
YES!!
Ha ha ha ha ha

Saturday, June 5
Sometimes I worry that I'm a robot and don't know it.
Don't talk of love
Well I've heard the word before
It's sleeping in my memory
I won't disturb the slumber
of feelings that have died
If I never loved I never
would have cried
I am a rock
I am an island
Get me out of here!!!!! This is crazy-town!!!!!
HONK HONK
Slobber
GLARE
YOU HONK WE DRINK!
Mean neighbors drove a truck onto their lawn and partied loudly for the entire day.
Thumpa-
thump thump
AAAAAOOO
thump
thumpa
Hippie communes down the alley from my house formed a massive drumcircle.
I am be—autifu-l in eeeeevery si—ngle waAAAaay!!
Neighbor riffed Christina Aguilera loudly out her window for an hour.

Sunday, June 6

I drew all day today.

I did not leave my house.

Arizona has been in the news and in online discussions a lot lately for blatant, horrid cases of racism bubbling up in rapid succession. It's made me spend a lot of time thinking about what makes people think and act that way.

I think it's very American to imagine oneself as an individual, or an island, and to glorify independence. When people think about themselves that way, and don't see how they are connected to everyone else, they have an easier time justifying hurting others.

However, independence is a delusion. We rely upon each other for everything, every day. What's so special about humans as a species is our ability to cooperate. Hurting another person hurts the whole, and will only hurt you in the end.

(You know, all of this being beside the fact that it is RIDICULOUS to hate based on race).

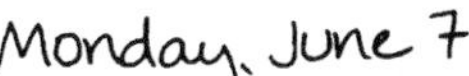
Monday, June 7

My room is very bright in the morning, to the point that I wore sunglasses today while toning!
MK
Too. Cool.

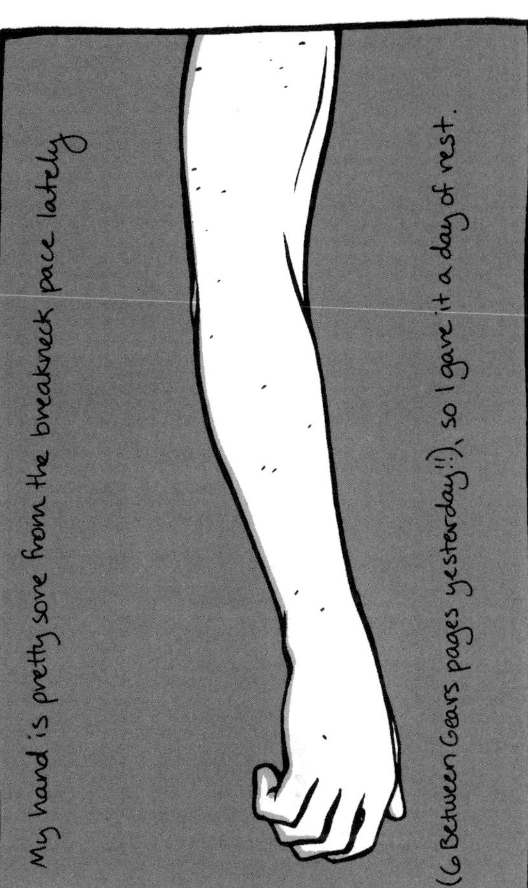
My hand is pretty sore from the breakneck pace lately
(6 Between Gears pages yesterday!), so I gave it a day of rest.

Printed huuuundreds of pages today in the library over 3 hours. I want to stock up on minicomics before I lose access to the UO and its cheap printing!

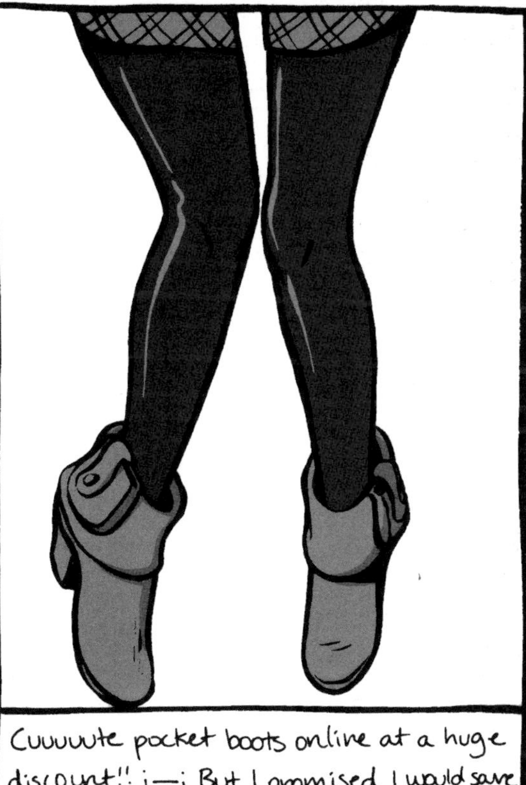
Cuuuute pocket boots online at a huge discount!! i—i But I promised I would save my money for high-quality things that I really need... and moving out of home sooner.

Tuesday, June 8

Boys living in our house next year came over to look at furniture. One of them bought my bed! Yaaaaaay! I might be able to move out in a single car trip!

Laundry.

Cooking pasta.

WOW. Only 4 more dinners in this house . . . .

Backing up hard drive.

Oh God ... it's been since February?!!

Fell asleep listening to the rain and a cat meowing to be let inside next door.

I dreamed that I lived there and I owned that cat, and I rushed to the door and scooped it up and dried it off and hugged it.

I really need a cat in my life again, huh?

Wednesday, June 9
I am so absent-minded lately! I only shaved one of my legs in the shower!
DAMN it!
prickle!
More summer rain today. The weather this year! Shape up, Oregon!
Soooooo lazy! I was supposed to do my take-home final today and finish a painting for a friend, but I didn't get started until 5:00. x __ x
Damn you, internet! So much more interesting than school...
You had better WATCH yourself...
PrADA members stick up for each other!

Thursday, June 10

Sent my take-home final to Professor Freedman! I am officially done with college!!!
Sketched some ideas for what I want my living space to be next year. I have decided that I am DEAD SET on having a comfy, reclining chair for reading. Random right? But I sorely missed comfy seating this year.
Ah! AHH!! What is this?!
What's dangerous??
What should I do?!!?
一人じゃない, LONG ♫ WAY HOME ♪
My head is a box filled with nothing and that's the way I like it
Last work out at the UO Rec Center!
Last John Henry's 80's Night! Followed by donuts from Voodoo. Choice evening. ☆

Friday, June 11

Last thing I remember before waking up: being ambushed by bad guys with chain cannons!
!!!

BUT THEN WHAT HAPPENS?!!
THUMP
THUMP
THUMP
I fell back to sleep, but didn't get a conclusion. :(

Watched TLC with Hannah, Christina, Chris, and Danielle until early afternoon.
This in an excellent hangover activity.

Couldn't get motivated to work on the art projects I am supposed to be doing. I normally don't let myself do other projects when I feel this way; I force myself to get through it, but today I let myself call it a wash and just worked on a fun illustration from start to finish.

Walked to Safeway after dark just to get out of the house. Bought random groceries for the last 2 days in Eugene and tooth whitener.
It's $30, but...

Saturday, June 12

Went to the Clothes Horse for the last time with Hannah. Bought a cute work outfit – patterned Anne Taylor top and black belted skirt ♡

Got frappuccinos and walked around 13th.

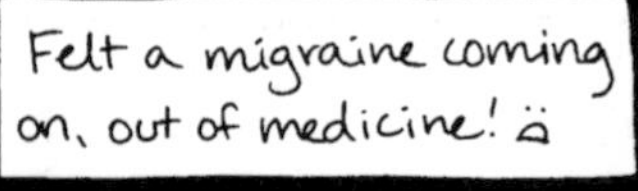
Felt a migraine coming on, out of medicine! ☹

Think of warming your hands by a fire... relax your face... try to sleep....
It worked, but I was scared. I have to get another pre-scription for abortive meds.

Slept for 12 hours, but woke up a couple of times in the middle.
I can't believe I graduate tomorrow!

Sunday, June 13

Woke up and started packing. My room has an echo!
weird...

Mom, Dad, Nick, Neil, and Grandma and Grandpa Blackwell came for dinner and to see me walk in the Honors College graduation ceremony.
Don't trip
clap
Don't trip
clap
Clap clap
clap
Don't trip
clap
clap clap
Clap clap
CHAMPAGNE!
Congratulations!!
Thank you!
internshi in Spain
Mom, you know Amelie and Niha?
What are you doing this summer?
going to miss it.
Picture!

WHAT
Mom and Dad are paying for me to visit Heather in New York this fall, and Grandma and Grandpa gave me a huuuge check to help me start my independent life! Savings goal reached!

Actual partying
We partied!
We did!
1 beer each
And I didn't even finish mine because I was DD.

I'm gonna miss this sooooo much!
Last Rennie's nachos ♡♡

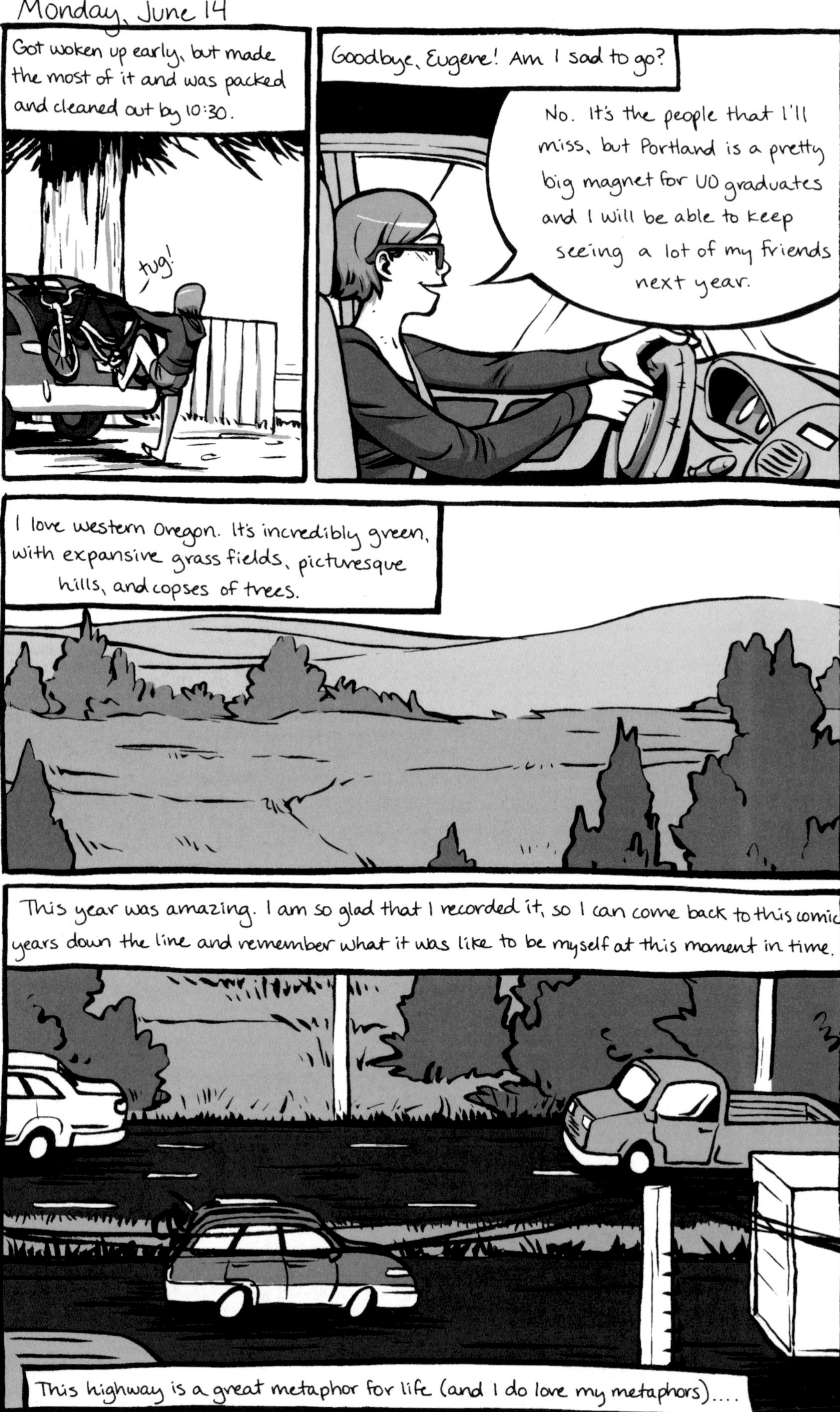
Monday, June 14
Got woken up early, but made the most of it and was packed and cleaned out by 10:30.
tug!
Goodbye, Eugene! Am I sad to go?
No. It's the people that I'll miss, but Portland is a pretty big magnet for UO graduates and I will be able to keep seeing a lot of my friends next year.
I love western Oregon. It's incredibly green, with expansive grass fields, picturesque hills, and copses of trees.
This year was amazing. I am so glad that I recorded it, so I can come back to this comic years down the line and remember what it was like to be myself at this moment in time.
This highway is a great metaphor for life (and I do love my metaphors)....

My experience driving between exits 194 and 292 will be uniquely mine, but I am traveling a road that millions have taken before me.
I will see the same landscape that countless others have seen, and though things change little by little, the truth is that I am connected to everyone who has ever seen these sights, taken these bumps, and gripped the wheel before me.
I can't see where the highway starts or ends, but the people around me and the people around them extend into a network that covers the entire road.
I am a part of the whole of that experience.
Thank you for traveling this stretch of the highway with me.
–Tally

BONUS MATERIAL

Process Notes

PLANNING: I started with a pretty basic concept: limited time-frame autobio comic about my senior year of college. It wasn't much of a leap to imagine that I would face preparations for graduation and job searching in that time.

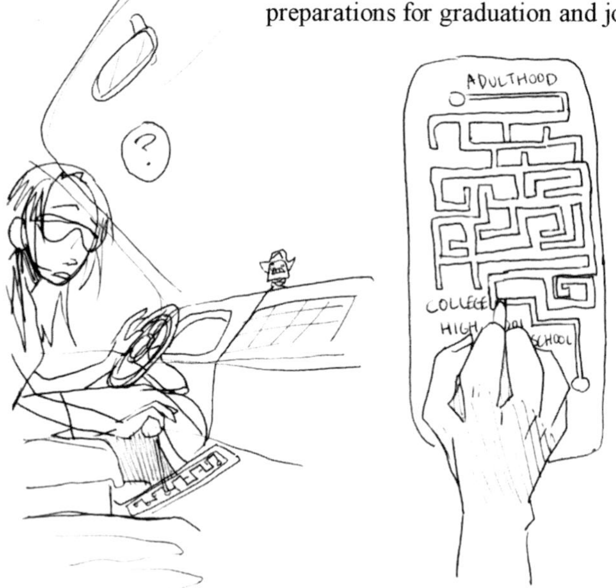
?
ADULTHOOD
COLLEGE
HIGH
SCHOOL

'Between Gears' came from the idiom of being a little lost between two things (for me, a predictable 19 years of school and what I assumed adult life was supposed to be). I played around with the idea of wanting to shift into the 'adulthood' gear, but things getting hopelessly complicated after you enter college. It feels less and less like there is a straight path you can follow and expect to be rewarded for following.

One thing I could do to prepare for the comic over the summer before it began was practice drawing myself. Honestly, it took a long time to pick out the features I thought were most recognizable and learn how to exaggerate them consistently. Looking back, it's hilarious how much time I spent practicing that hair cut, since I chopped it off two days into the comic!

GLUG
GLUG
GLUG
Ahh.
Just a little more...
SPLATTER

I had some ideas for structural elements before beginning the comic. For example, I thought I would have several exaggerated versions of myself: sorority girl, nerd, honors student, comic artist, inner 7-year-old, and bitch, who would duke it out when I had internal conflicts and pop up for comedic effect when a certain side of me came out.

sorority girl
power user
HC student
Comic Artist
I'm not going to grow up.
Yes you are.
Between Gears

By the time I began drawing, though, I felt that it was a labored and shallow idea, so I axed it.

I also thought about the span of the project -- 9 months -- and tried to make a pregnancy allegory, but that was even worse!

My advice to anyone who wants to try autobio comics is that this is a worthwhile exercise, but you should be open to scrapping these ideas and letting things evolve naturally. I found that I needed ‘lazy side’ and ‘responsible side’ to describe the way that I was feeling, but I didn’t predict that. You’ll accumulate your personal language for these things if you give it time, experiment, and let it come to you.

The summer before Between Gears began, I drew a test page for a random day to practice turning a day into a comic page. I didn't take it too seriously, just tried it and then stepped back to look at the results. Between Gears was different enough from other projects I had done to warrant some practice and preparation.

Testing, testing...
I woke up very late today, and I woke up VERY SICK.
Oo.. ..Ooooh...
stuffy nose, cloudy head, sore throat! Sad Tally
which was maybe not the best state of mind for transferring all of my files to my new laptop
I do what now?
Hit... enter...
patient Dad
The cleaners came a day early, which only bothered me because I am doing a painting for Joe, and thought it needed another day of work.
But he said:
I love it!
which was a relief.
I've become addicted to Tetris. Today, I set up an account on Tetris Friends!!! Nick says it leads to paranoia and violence, but I think carpal tunnel will come first.
KL CKALAK
I got extremely confrontational and touchy at dinner tonight.
You're calling a 14-year-old girl "hot"!!
BAM
But a couple episodes of the Office had us in a better mood soon.
I'm not eloquent with these things that bother me. I started talking nonsense and lost my point.
- Woke up late, sick
- Loaded laptop w/ Dad
- Cleaners came
- Showed Joe the painting
- Addicted to Tetris
- Got huffy at dinner
- Watched The Office, Burn Notice, movies w/ Nick

From this exercise, I learned that I would probably need to thumbnail pages rather than go straight to drawing them. I needed some help visualizing the page before I began drawing, as evidenced by the panels that didn't make it in, the text box outside of the last panel, and the many cramped word balloons.

THERE ARE ALWAYS A MILLION REASONS NOT TO START A PERSONAL PROJECT. MINE FOR NOT KEEPING A COMIC DIARY WERE:
I'M TOO BUSY.
...
I SHOULD WAIT 'TIL I'M BETTER.
IT'S BEEN DONE BEFORE.
and better
BUT STILL, I FELT THE TUG TO START AN ILLUSTRATED JOURNAL AGAIN AND AGAIN. AND REALLY, PERSONAL PROJECTS ARE PERSONAL BECAUSE WE DO THEM FOR OURSELVES, NOT LOGIC.
OKAY. THAT'S ENOUGH.
I'VE BEEN WANTING TO DO THIS, AND IT'S TIME I *STARTED.*

Another test page, I tried to draw this completely seriously, as if it was for the comic (I used it as a teaser the month before the comic began). I always do a test run with my final materials before starting a project -- I have to know how it will look before I commit, and make sure that there isn't a conflict between any of my materials. In this case, that proved to be a very good choice, since I did not like the look of computer-generated lettering and decided after seeing this to hand-letter.

Creating Pages

Each page of Between Gears went through 5 stages to reach completion: notes, thumbnails, pencils, inks, and tones.

Notes: I took notes about every day in a Word document that got to be 200+ pages long as I fell farther and farther behind on Between Gears. Here is an example of one day's worth of notes:

> Sunday, April 11, 2010
>
> -Thesis countdown: 23 days, 20 comic pages remaining
>
> -Talked to Dad about the contract I got last week. He gave me tips for writing my reply email.
>
> -He also gave me his opinion on my JET decision: "You'll have your whole life to travel. This is not travel. This is an intensive cultural immersion. Ask yourself how worthwhile that is, given your length of study with Japan already."
>
> -Walked to the grocery store and back for a little exercise and fresh air.
>
> -Called home and talked to the family. "We're in the middle of LOST!" "Ooooh! Okay, no spoilers, BUT IT'S THE BEST ONE OF THE SEASON!"

Thumbnails: Next comes a very small rough draft of the page based on the notes. This stage is all about deciding what information is important and laying out where each panel will go on the page. At this stage, I sometimes choose to cut things that there isn't room for, or add panels if something needs more room to be clear.

Sat April 10
OH NO
quote
Sun April 11

Pencils: Next, I draw my for-reals page at full size with non-photo blue lead in a mechanical pencil. Because of this, I have no penciled page to show as an example! I love non-photo blue lead because I can ink right over my pencils and don't need to erase anything afterward; scanners can't pick up the blue and it saves me a lot of time.

Inks: I inked Between Gears with a Pentel pocket brush pen. It's a fantastic tool; it dries quickly, has no clean-up, and simulates a real brush pretty well with synthetic bristles. I inked some details and lettered with microns (I discovered the Pilot VBall BeGreen pen in the middle of the project and it is my new favorite pen).

Sunday, April 11
Thesis countdown: 23 days, 20 comic pages remaining.
Talked to Dad about contracts. He gave me tips for writing counter-proposals.
Uh-huh. OK.
He also gave me his opinion about JET (again).
You'll have your whole life to travel. This is not travel. This is an intensive cultural immersion. Ask yourself how worthwhile that is, given your length of study with Japan already.
Walked to the grocery store and back for a little exercise and fresh air.
Called home and talked to the family.
We're in the middle of LOST!
Oooooh! Okay, no spoilers, but... IT'S THE BEST ONE OF THE SEASON!!

Tones: I scan my inked page and start to edit the digital file using my computer, a Wacom tablet, and Photoshop. I adjust levels, convert it to a bitmap, clean up the line art, convert it back to grayscale, and tone on a new layer (or two or three). The end result is a high-resolution image file that can be altered for web or print!

Sunday, April 11
Thesis countdown: 23 days, 20 comic pages remaining.
Talked to Dad about contracts. He gave me tips for writing counter-proposals.
Uh-huh. OK.
He also gave me his opinion about JET (again).
You'll have your whole life to travel. This is not travel. This is an intensive cultural immersion. Ask yourself how worthwhile that is, given your length of study with Japan already.
Walked to the grocery store and back for a little exercise and fresh air.
Called home and talked to the family.
We're in the middle of LOST!
Oooooh! Okay, no spoilers, but... IT'S THE BEST ONE OF THE SEASON!!

Frequently Asked Questions

Why did you choose to do this project?

I began thinking about tackling a big autobio project in early 2009. I was a junior in college looking for a topic to develop into my senior thesis, and I knew I wanted to draw a comic for it.

I was inspired by autobio authors like Emi Lenox, Erika Moen, Marc Ellerby, and Jennie Breeden. I loved how they had beautiful recordings of their lives that they could go back and read. I wanted something like that to remember my senior year by. I kept journals, but comics described the mood of events more accurately and concisely. I knew I was going to have to make some big decisions during the school year, and thought it would be a great framework for an autobio project.

In October, I decided that Between Gears wasn't right for the thesis. For one thing, it wouldn't really be done in May, when I needed to present my thesis. For another, autobio didn't represent my work to date, or what I wanted to pursue in the future. It was a short-term experiment. I decided that I needed to develop a work of fiction for the thesis, which is where Over the Surface came from. I continued Between Gears, though, for my own enjoyment and for the sake of experimentation.

What did you learn?

The biggest difference I notice between early and late Between Gears pages is in the inking. I was just starting to use a brush pen in the summer of 2009 after inking with a nib for five years. They are very different tools! It took a lot of getting used to. By the later pages, which were drawn in 2011, I was comfortable with the brush pen and the strokes were less labored and messy.

Having to recall my day and record it later made me more observant as I went through life. If something was funny, I repeated it in my head several times immediately after and committed it to memory. If there was someone I was going to need to draw later, I made mental notes of their defining features. I thought all day about comics and how I would turn my experiences into comics.

What did you enjoy the most?

Between Gears was totally up to me and it was very liberating. I had some guidelines for how autobio worked based on the autobio comics I was reading, but I didn't feel restricted by much beyond 'one page for every day' (which I broke in the end anyway!). I tried tons of new things, failed, succeeded, and learned. I had a rule against using rulers -- I didn't want to put any pressure on myself that would scare me away from drawing a page. I didn't draw backgrounds or crowds when I didn't want to. I wanted to see Between Gears as a book when it was done, but I didn't let myself worry about how publishers or anyone else would view it. It was very fun to draw for myself.

Also, I love love LOVE drawing extreme expressions, and this project let me play with that on pretty much every page.

What did you like the least? What was the hardest?

Caricatures were frustrating. I think I got better with practice, but if people didn't have distinctive hairstyles, I struggled with differentiating their faces and body shapes enough to communicate who they were supposed to be.

Another challenge was how far behind I fell. I think I was only drawing pages within a week of them happening through October, and then I fell steadily further and further behind. I took detailed notes for each day, but often forgot to include things like what I was wearing or what the weather was like, so I had to do some guessing when I drew pages a year after the fact. It's a detail, but I wanted Between Gears to be as accurate as possible!

I also struggled with the line between being honest and being respectful of people who make appearances in Between Gears. The relationship with Nate is the most obvious example, but there was also Amélie, who was running for student body president and maybe didn't want her house parties documented, and several other cases. I asked permission when I wanted to show something but wasn't sure if people involved would be comfortable with it.

Will you do autobio again?

If something really interesting happened to me, I could see doing another finite project, but I would have to have a purpose/framework from the beginning, and it would probably be shorter than Between Gears. (I think it would be cool to repeat the experiment in another 21 years, or if I have a child in his or her senior year of college, and see how differently it turned out...) I am really, REALLY glad I did this comic, and would absolutely do it again given the choice, but right now I am really excited to get back into fiction.

That said, I *do* enjoy recording jokes and little moments from life in quick comics. I often use my 20-minute commute to Periscope as a window to create a short autobio comic. Trying to draw something quickly and not get too caught up in the details is an interesting challenge.

There was a guy who walked past the bus stop carrying a broom.
I kind of hoped he was a dude-witch
At the Rose Festival with Molly:
IS THAT CENTRIFUGAL FORCE
AHA HA
HA-HA
HA HA!
AAAAA!
HA HA
HA!
HA
HA
OR ARE YOU JUST HAPPY TO SEE ME?
THE SCRAMBLER
How are you with animals and your proximity to them?
Yes?

Do you mind if I ask where you got your purse?
Forever 21!
It's cute!
I know!
...
'I know'?!! Try 'thank you' next time.

In the locker room, my foot caught on my gym bag and tripped me.
whoops.
It should have been easy to correct, but...
We had done so many kicking drills in class that night...
The muscles that pull my leg up were completely spent.
So I just ate shit.

Oh great, there's a spider on the ceiling. Now I'll be thinking about it and not relaxing
skitter
WHAT NO STAY OVER THERE
AUGH! STOP DOING WHAT YOU ARE DOING!

Dear man at the gym who caught a medicine ball and shouted:
IT'S SO FLUFFY!!
...You are my favorite.

LOOFAH'D
SHAMPOO SMUSH
glance
glance
SHUDDER

Kim Kardashian is pregnant, with what we can only hope is a human child.
Really? I can think of a lot of things I'd rather it was than another Kardashian.

Like a Face-hugger.

I also like to make comics to remember trips by. It's easy to forget inside jokes and the way you feel in a certain moment, but making comics real-time on a trip commits them pretty solidly to memory.

Here are several comics from my San Francisco graduation roadtrip:

The Redwoods part 1
Ginormous uprooted redwood
WOW!
It kind of reminds me of a space worm that comes out and swallows spaceships...
Well, I wasn't going to admit it, but that's totally the first thing I thought of, too.
I love that we are nerds
Lucky us
Okay, so this is kind of funny... We're on the '14th' floor, otherwise known as.....
...
OOOOH.
Yeah.
You should write comics
After-dinner walk...
Is that...a cave?
Spooky!
FLASH
If this was a movie, you would have just taken a picture of whatever lives in that cave...
...
...And it would come after you tonight to destroy the evidence!
WHY WOULD YOU SAY THAT?!
easily freaked out
My dream from last night
The house is on fire! Everybody get out!!!!
Where's ____??
He faxed himself to us.
Hey guys!
WHAT GOOD IS THIS?!!!?!

That's what you get for being a butterfly.
Mom is really good at spotting wildlife.
Elk!
Salamander!
Trails are better left to me.
Do you think the trail goes down to the beach?
No.
TRAIL
Pretty view in Trinidad Bay B+B
I drew this a little bit drunk.
My dreams, let me show you them
The lava is coming.
Oh no!!
Our puppies will never get to know each other...!
-Yip!
Oh Mom ♡
That's the first time that I've seen a US Bank flying a gay flag.
What is the gay flag?
CASTRO
...?
Did I say that Mom and I are nerds...?
Nick is on a Harry Potter kick
...Yesterday I realized that the only HP movie I haven't seen is the 3rd one.
Oh, really? It's good!
Oh no, I know. I mean it's the only one I haven't seen in the last 48 hours.
...

What came after that year?

...Are you ready for this?

...When the portal opened up ahead of me, there was barely time to blink.
I found myself in an alternate existence where there was no respite from the internecine horrors of radiation clouds, arcane cyborgs, and flesh-eating mutants.
After my first few scrapes with the self-appointed lords of this wicked hellscape, I discovered why they brought me here.
They had scanned the multiverse and found a discrepancy; in their world a 'Natalie Nourigat' was never born. Their goal there-after was to capture me and remake their globe with the secrets stored in my 'existence pattern'.
It was clear that, in my absence, my own Earth would descend into a mirror image of this flailing, perpetual carnival of gore and adrenaline.
BASE 47
That was a year ago.
I've since learned how to hold my own against the wretched hoards and more importantly...
how to get back and prevent this fate for the other realms and other Natalies spanning the time-space domain.

The last of their 7 dimensional punch gates wasn't easy to find; they had become desperate and moved it underground.
Without a working model to retro-engineer they will remain sealed away forever.
First I'd use it to make an escape-tunnel and end this obscene detour into the world's worst of reality's boondocks!
I could hear the claws on the rusty steel flooring.
I entered the cosmos-code for Periscope Studio.
I just hope I'm not too late to save my home world...

Here are some pages from the Between Gears minicomic that I put together for conventions in spring of 2010.

"My favorite part of comics is drawing fun expressions. This project has been so great for that, because I can stretch my face as extremely as I want, and offend no one but me!"

EXPRESSION PAGE
blink
blink
MU-
HA
HA
...
HMM

SONGS
used in
Between Gears

Sep 17: Remember You're a Girl by Kaiser Chiefs
Sep 22: Secret Tunnel from Avatar the Last Airbender
Sep 24: Living on a Prayer by Bon Jovi
Oct 8: Jumpin Jumpin by Destiny's Child
Oct 13: Armchairs by Andrew Bird
Oct 16: Sloths from the SNL Digital Short
Oct 24: Theme from Inspector Gadget
Dec 4: Sooner or Later by Fastball
Dec 9: The Circle of Life from The Lion King
Dec 27: 1901 by Phoenix
Dec 28: You by Atmosphere
Jan 13: I Wanna Be Like You performed by (you love it) Smash Mouth
Jan 16: It Had Better Be Tonight performed by Michael Bublé
Jan 21: Until the End by Norah Jones
Jan 26: Cherry Lips by Garbage
Feb 6: Oh My Ghost by Betty and the Boy
Feb 7: Prison Girls by Neko Case
Feb 9: Living on a Prayer by Bon Jovi (yes twice)
Feb 17: Fabulous from High School Musical 2
Feb 18: For the Longest Time by Billy Joel
Feb 23: Step by Step by Whitney Houston
Feb 25: Hot by Missy Elliot (Ratatat remix)
Feb 26: Bad Romance by Lady Gaga
Feb 27: Kodoku no SIGNAL from Serial Experiments LAIN
Feb 28: Muscle Museum by Muse

Mar 1: Bop to the Top from High School Musical
Mar 2: I'm Your Daddy by Weezer
Mar 3: Lasso by Phoenix
Mar 4: Ashes by Embrace
Mar 8: Stylo by Gorillaz
Mar 10: Handlebars by Flobots
Mar 15: Short Skirt Long Jacket by Cake
Mar 17: Dominos by The Big Pink
Mar 18: Closer by Nine Inch Nails
Mar 22: Old Time Rock & Roll by Bob Seger
April 1: In My Place by Coldplay
Apr 26: Bet On It from High School Musical 2
Natalie by Florez
I Could Say by Lily Allen
Almost There from The Princess and the Frog
Apr 29: Hoodoo by Muse
May 10: Umi no Okaasan from Ponyo on the Cliff by the Sea
May 11: Step by Step by Whitney Houston (YES TWICE)
May 19 and 20: Theme Song from Pokemon
May 25: Just A Girl by No Doubt
Jun 3: What Time Is It? from High School Musical 2
Jun 5: I am a Rock by Simon and Garfunkle
Beautiful by Christina Aguilera
Jun 10: Long Way Home by SPEED
Catch My Disease by Ben Lee

DO NOT ATTEMPT

Finally...

I wanted to take a little more space to say thank you for picking up this book. I hope that you enjoyed reading Between Gears as much as I enjoyed making it.

Thank you to Eric Stephenson for giving Between Gears a chance, and to everyone at Image for making it look good and getting it into people's hands!

Thank you to the University of Oregon, the Robert D. Clark Honors College, and Pi Beta Phi for four years of great memories.

Thank you to Molly Muldoon for showing up in a truck and making things better whenever she is needed.

Thank you to Ben Dewey for creating *Nourigeddon* and for being an excellent friend and human being.

Special thanks to Emi Lenox, Jamie S. Rich, Hope Larson, George Rohac, Drew Gill, Jeff Parker, Erika Moen, and everyone at Periscope who gave me book advice.

Natalie moved back in with her parents after graduation. She went on a lovely road trip to San Francisco with her mother, worked a summer job at the Oregon Zoo, became financially independent, and moved into a cute, ancient apartment with Hannah in NW Portland. She visited Heather in NYC and attended New York Comic-Con. She created a series of children's books with her father and drew two graphic novels for publishers. She joined Periscope Studio, took up French and karate classes, and adopted a cat.

She is currently very happy.

Visit www.NatalieNourigat.com for more artwork and news about future projects.

3/12 GRAPHIC

FOREST

Joëlle

Jamie

Pollution Factory Land

30

Will... Riv...

Laika

PORTLAND STREETCAR

Pearl District

NOB HILL

NW 23rd Ave (shopping!)

NW 21st Ave (bars!)

Uni... (bu...

Pittock Mansion

hobos

Coffee Time

405

Stacks of money

Silk

dogs dogs dogs

EMITOWN

Sushi La...

BURNSIDE

Coffee House NW

Powell's

Rose Gardens

PGE Park

Multnomah Athletic Club

MAX

Reading Frenzy

WEST HILLS

GOOSE HOLLOW

Lincoln High School

Pioneer

DOWNT...

Park Blocks

Tunnel!

PSU

26

Oregon Zoo

MAX

Expensive Hill Houses

Home

Med Students

Terw...

Space Hospital

Hillsdale

E...